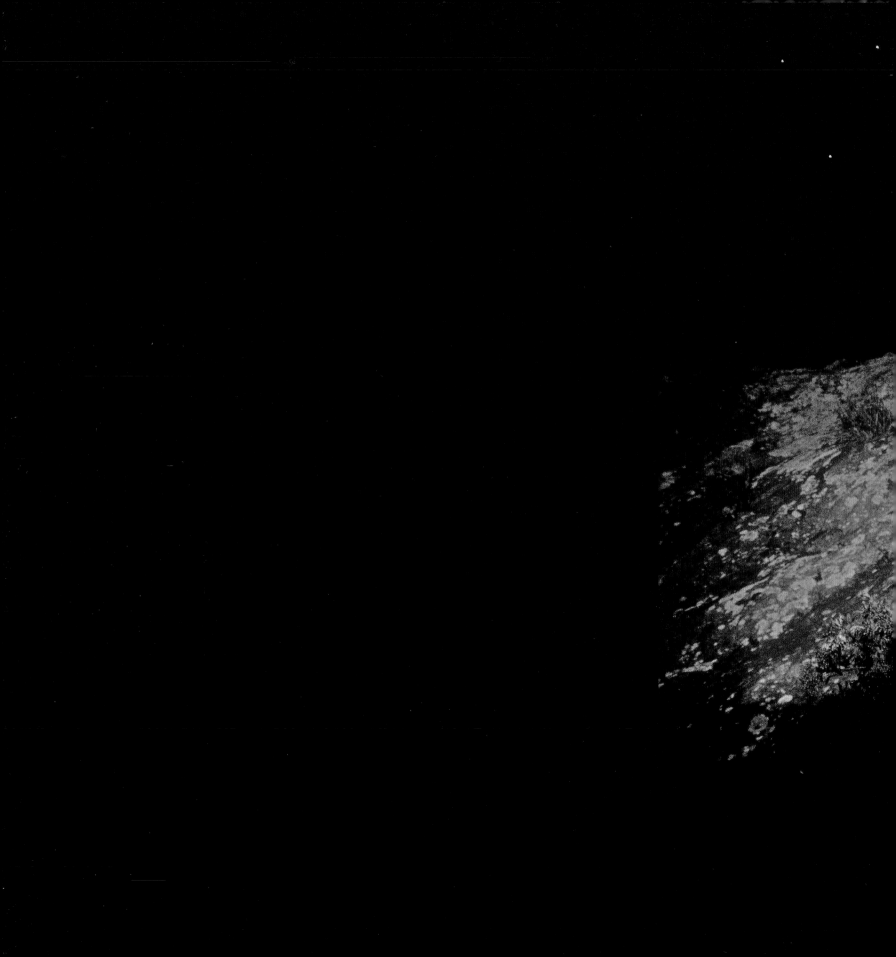

BERKELEY ROCKS

BERKELEY ROCKS

BUILDING WITH NATURE

JONATHAN CHESTER

TEXT BY DAVE WEINSTEIN

TEN SPEED PRESS
Berkeley | Toronto

Ten Speed Press

PO Box 7123

Berkeley, CA 94707

Distributed in Australia by Simon and Schuster Australia, in Canada by Ten Speed Press Canada, in New Zealand by Southern Publishers Group, in South Africa by Real Books, and in the United Kingdom and Europe by Publishers Group UK.

Cover and book design by Nancy Austin

Maps by Bart Wright

Captions for photos on preceding pages:

Page i: A section of the mysterious rock walls (discussed on page 39) can be found just east of the Seaview trail on the north side of Tilden Park's Vollmer Peak.

Page ii: This massive boulder hidden in leafy Kensington inspired this book.

Page iv: Looking toward Albany Hill from Indian Rock.

Page vi: A giant rock dominates a yard on Vincente Avenue in north Berkeley.

Page x: A view of Shasta Rock in Thousand Oaks.

Library of Congress Cataloging-in-Publication Data

Chester, Jonathan.

  Berkeley rocks : building with nature / Jonathan Chester ; text by Dave Weinstein.

    p. cm.

  Includes bibliographical references and index.

  ISBN-13: 978-1-58008-486-4 (hardcover : alk. paper)

  ISBN-10: 1-58008-486-9 (hardcover : alk. paper)

  1. Geology--California--Berkeley Hills. 2. Volcanic ash, tuff, etc.--California--Berkeley Hills. 3. Volcanic ash, tuff, etc.--California--Berkeley Hills--Pictorial works. 4. Berkeley Hills (Calif.)--History. I. Title.

  QE90.B454C44 2006

  557.94'65--dc22

                      2006023543

First printing, 2006

Printed in China

1 2 3 4 5 6 7 8 9 10 — 10 09 08 07 06

To Kirsty, Katharine, and Cormac

CONTENTS

Indian Rock, the most famous of Berkeley's public rocks, has seen many eras of human appreciation. It was a place of shelter and congregation in the days of the Ohlone, and remains a popular gathering spot for those hungry for a good view of the Bay. The steps carved into Indian Rock (possibly as a WPA project in the 1930s) facilitate easier access to the summit and glorious view. These same steps also provide a safe descent route for the many climbers who tackle the challenging boulder problems on the rock's back face.

INTRODUCTION

WHEN BERKELEY WAS NEW, rocks dominated the scene. They towered thirty feet or more above the grassy oak woodlands and could be seen from across the Bay. Today, though just as tall and imposing, the rocks have retreated from view—so much so that many people have only the vaguest notion they exist.

West of Colusa Avenue, an oak-shaded thoroughfare that separates the flatlands from the hills, you'll find a mere handful of elephant-sized rocks, some of them incorporated into a bus stop. But east of Colusa, just steps away, is another world—that of the Berkeley Rocks.

Immense crags form miniature mountains in many yards. Vincente Avenue is so jammed with rocks that nearly every house has one, some prominently displayed in front, others actually inside the houses, filling up garages and serving as foundations. Some of the largest hide in backyards, where they loom two or three stories tall yet remain invisible from the road.

Adding to the romance of the rocks is the drama surrounding their origin. Geologically, California is as complicated as it gets, a mélange of stone, mud, and the lithified remains of dead sea creatures. This mélange was shoved against the side of North America 155 million years ago, then

Embracing a beautiful boulder-strewn knoll on Brewster Street in El Cerrito, this
Japanese-influenced house is a superb example of building with nature.

1

Left: Rambling gardens and rocks are the perfect foreground match for views of San Francisco Bay.

Below: Certain rocks with just the right texture, dimensions, and character become outdoor gyms for the subset of rock climbers who practice bouldering.

tumbled and scrambled, and topped by volcanic flows that settled onto the earth like chocolate sauce on ice cream, then scrambled some more.

Berkeley's rocks seem to flow like a wave or like something alive, dipping beneath the earth and hiding in basements, only to emerge at a distance, sinuous, gliding downhill toward the Bay.

Rock-strewn hills can be found throughout the Bay Area. What makes the Berkeley Rocks truly special is what the people of Berkeley and surrounding towns have done with them.

The sidewalk on the edge of The Alameda in Thousand Oaks flows around the rocks.

They have come to love the rocks and have built up among them one of the loveliest yet craggiest neighborhoods in the world, one imbued with the principles of the Arts and Crafts movement, which were current when Berkeley began moving into its hills. Builders were influenced by architects, landscapers, designers, and theorists of what we call the First, Second, and Third Bay Traditions, and they sought to provide dwellings in harmony with nature.

From the start, the rocks played an important part. "Consider a spot upon the slope of the foothills, where the ground is rendered unavailable for agricultural pursuits by the steep inclines

The train/trolley car system had tracks that followed the contours of the hills. This transportation network helped open up the Cragmont subdivision of north Berkeley, billed as a "park dotted with homes," to development around 1907.

or by the frequent outcroppings of rock, but where gnarled oaks spread their distorted branches and serpent-like roots on every hand," wrote Mark Daniels, the landscape designer and architect who helped lay out the Thousand Oaks neighborhood, in an article "California as a Place of Homes" for the July 1915 issue of *California Magazine*. "Here is an ideal location for landscape architecture."

Walking the hills today shows how right Daniels was. You'll find immense rocks impinging on sidewalks and other rocks that determined the route of roadways. You'll find rocks that are natural and in place, some that are natural but displaced, "dry walls" of local stone put together without mortar, and walls that are mortared.

Public paths, ranging from concrete steps bordered by elegant balustrades to dirt trails, lace the Berkeley Hills, providing excellent opportunities to peer into people's backyards. Many reveal decades-old outdoor stone fireplaces, once central to family entertainment but today largely ignored.

This stone fireplace (in what was originally the garden of the Spring Mansion on San Antonio Avenue) was once one of many such outdoor structures made of local rhyolite.

Many rocks are shaded by live oaks, their limbs snaking over the rocky surface and echoing its shape. A surprising number of oaks grow directly from the rocks. Exotic trees—red maples, eucalyptus, redwoods from the coast—shade many rocks. But enough live oaks remain to suggest what the area looked like before settlers made their mark on the land.

Charles Keeler, a Berkeley poet, naturalist, and prophet of the good life who wrote *The Simple Home* at the start of the twentieth century, envisioned a neighborhood filled with woodsy homes that blended with the landscape. What we have instead is a streetscape far more varied, larded with houses that pretend to be French Norman or Old English or Spanish hacienda, and others that would blend unobtrusively into a neighborhood in Vienna or a beachside cliff on the Sonoma coast. Yet how well they work with the rocks!

Occasionally you come upon a house and garden so shaved and civilized that it doesn't fit. It seems the antithesis of what the Berkeley Hills are all about: a landscape made of fire and flow.

"Here is an ideal location for landscape architecture"—
a landscape of fire and flow.

A SIMPLE HOUSE

"We who would have new life must do as the flowers do—must dwell with Nature and let her rains fall upon us and her sun shine on our heads; must listen to the singing of her birds, and stand in the presence of her trees," Charles Keeler advised readers of the *Overland Monthly* in December 1899. "Then shall we be reborn into a new life and uplifted into a new heaven upon earth. When we walk the fields by day the flowers shall lift their heads and speak to us, and when we go abroad at night we shall hear the music of the spheres."

It's not surprising that the author of these words—the man who proselytized for the simple home and was friends with naturalists John Burroughs and John Muir, as well as a member of a scientific expedition to the glaciers of Alaska and the inventor of a "universal religion," the Cosmic Society—would build himself a home atop a rock.

Keeler's house grows from a chunk of Leona rhyolite in Berkeley's Claremont district. The house began in 1907 as Keeler's studio, where he could write his poems for adults ("On Papeete Beach") and children ("Elfin Songs of Sunland"), essays ("Thoughts on Home Building in California"), a mystery play (*Triumph of Light*), and books about nature (*Summer Birds of the Redwoods*).

The studio was one-room and rustic, with an open-beamed ceiling, large fireplace, nooks and crannies, and small bays. Keeler used local stone to construct rock walls and a rock bridge across the creek that flows through the hilly site. He also built an amphitheater on the site using local stone.

Above: Charles Keeler's rustic studio.

Left: Charles Keeler: poet, philosopher, and author.

Keeler eventually moved into the studio, added a chaletlike addition, and lived there the rest of his life. On his death, in 1937, the *Berkeley Daily Gazette* called the home and theater "one of the show places of Berkeley."

Ann Luse, who lives in the Keeler house with her husband, Bob, remembers visiting it as a young girl. "It was like walking through a tunnel of oleander and wisteria all in bloom," she says. "It was the enchanted cottage."

The intimate connection between Charles Keeler's house and the rocks it is perched on is now obscured by vegetation.

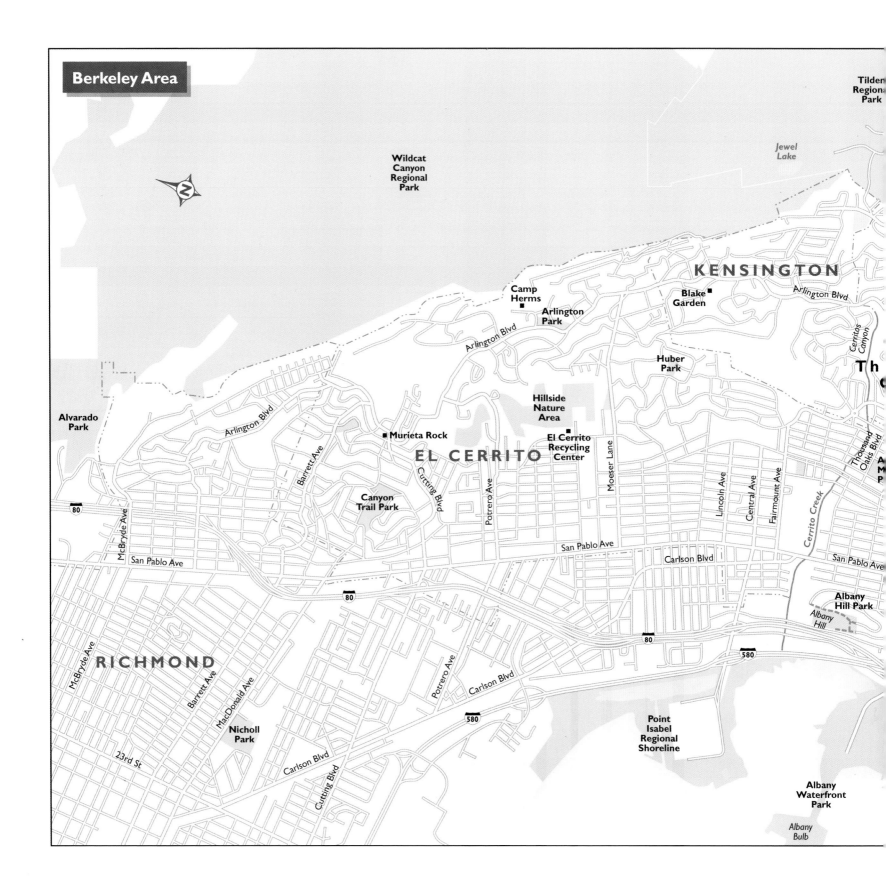

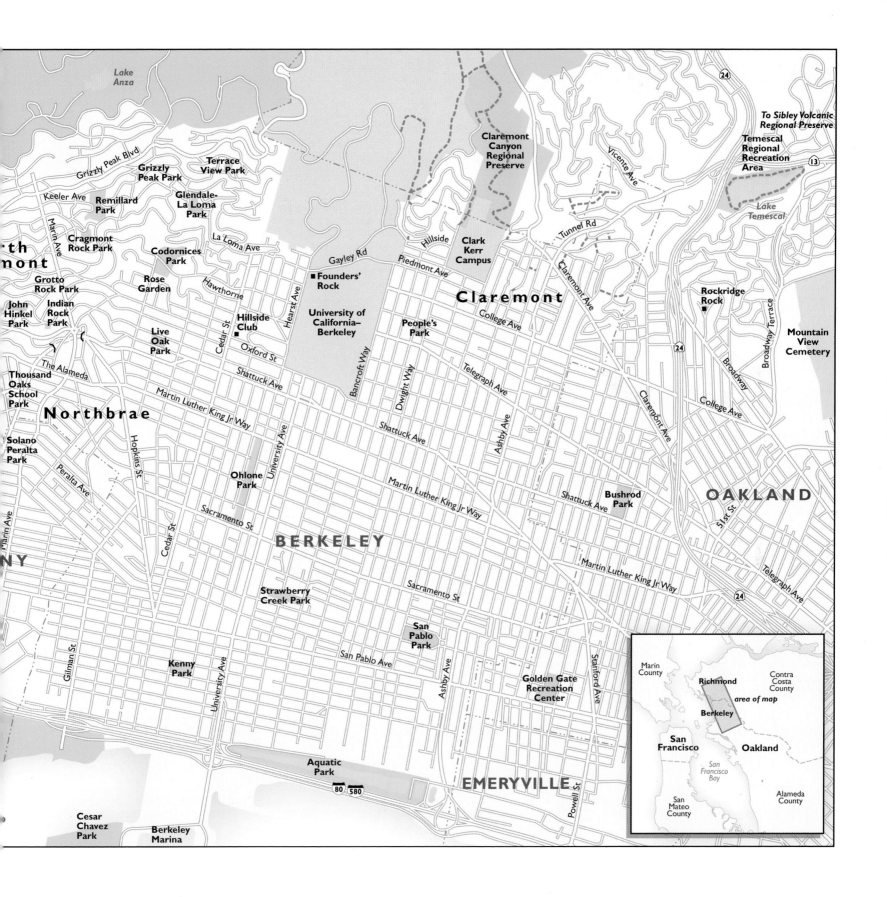

I. THE LAND BEFORE HUMANS

FOR MORE THAN A CENTURY, geologists have been pondering the Berkeley Rocks. What are they made of, how old are they, and where do they come from? None of these questions has been definitively answered, but much has been learned. "As new techniques are developing," says geologist Doris Sloan, author of *Geology of the San Francisco Bay Region*, "our understanding grows. It's fun that there are things we don't know yet."

As land masses go, California is relatively new—new in geologic time, that is. For the immense stretch of time from the earth's origins about 4.5 billion years ago up to just 200 million years ago, most of what we now know as California didn't exist. As recently as 140 million years ago, open sea crashed on the western shore of North America in the vicinity of today's Great Salt Lake.

Modern plate tectonic theory explains how California came to be. The earth's crust is divided into immense plates, many miles thick, that slowly move independently of one another. Oceanic plates are composed of denser rock, whereas the rocks of continental crust are lighter. Where these two types of plates meet, as on the west coast of North America, the heavier oceanic plate inevitably dives beneath the continental plate. But in the process, everything that could be found on the

Before urban settlement, the Berkeley Hills were mostly bare of trees.
Today, Wildcat Canyon gives a glimpse of how they once looked.

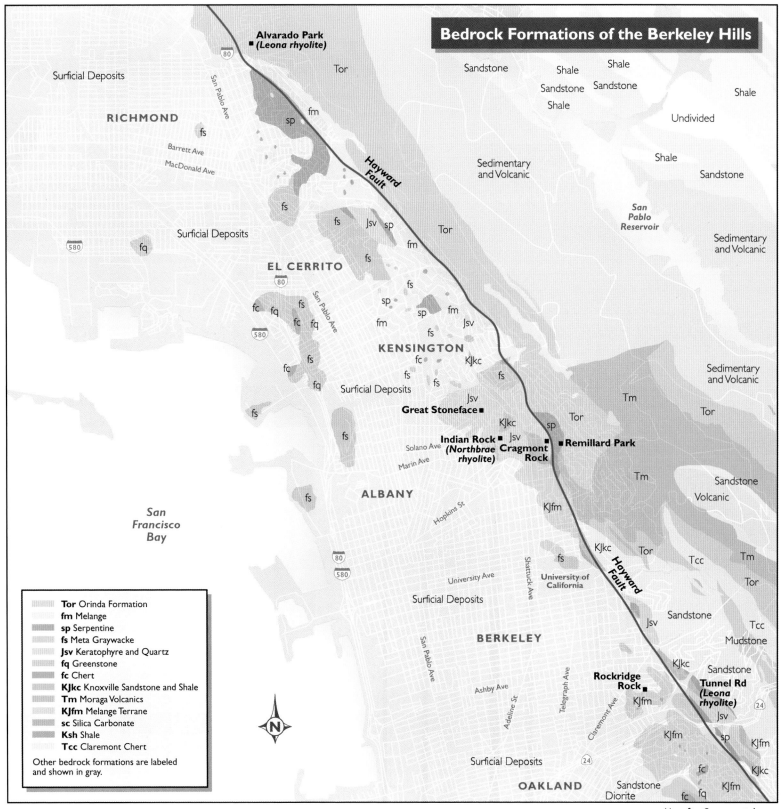

Bedrock Formations of the Berkeley Hills

Alvarado Park (*Leona rhyolite*)

Tor

Sandstone · Shale · Shale
Sandstone · Sandstone
Shale · Shale

Shale

Undivided

RICHMOND

Surficial Deposits

fs

Barrett Ave
MacDonald Ave

San Pablo Ave

fm
sp

Hayward Fault

Sedimentary and Volcanic

Shale

Sandstone

San Pablo Reservoir

Sedimentary and Volcanic

Surficial Deposits

fq

580

fs

fs · Jsv · sp
fm

Tor

EL CERRITO

80

fc · fq · fs
fc · fq
fq

San Pablo Ave

sp
fm
fs

sp
fs
Jsv

KENSINGTON

fc
KJkc

Sedimentary and Volcanic

fc

fs · fs
fq

Surficial Deposits

fs

Jsv

fs

Tm

Great Stoneface ■

KJkc
Jsv
Indian Rock ■ (*Northbrae rhyolite*)
Cragmont Rock
sp
Tor
Remillard Park ■

Tor

Solano Ave
Marin Ave

fs

ALBANY

KJfm

Tm

Sandstone
Volcanic

Hopkins St

San Francisco Bay

80
580

KJkc
Tor
Tcc
Tm

fs
University of California

University Ave

Shattuck Ave

Jsv
Sandstone
Tcc
Mudstone

San Pablo Ave

BERKELEY

KJkc

Sandstone

Ashby Ave

Telegraph Ave
Adeline St

Rockridge Rock ■

KJfm

Tunnel Rd (*Leona rhyolite*)

Jsv
sp
KJfm

Claremont Ave

KJfm

24

fc
fc · fq

KJkc
KJfm

Surficial Deposits

24

OAKLAND
Sandstone
Diorite

Legend:

	Tor	Orinda Formation
	fm	Melange
	sp	Serpentine
	fs	Meta Graywacke
	Jsv	Keratophyre and Quartz
	fq	Greenstone
	fc	Chert
	KJkc	Knoxville Sandstone and Shale
	Tm	Moraga Volcanics
	KJfm	Melange Terrane
	sc	Silica Carbonate
	Ksh	Shale
	Tcc	Claremont Chert

Other bedrock formations are labeled and shown in gray.

N

Map after Graymer, et al., 1995

floor of the ocean—sedimentary rocks formed from sand, from mud, and from dead microscopic sea creatures, plus volcanic boulders and debris of all kinds—is scraped off onto the edge of the continent.

One result of these processes is California, which not all geologists find entirely pretty. In their book *Roadside Geology of Northern and Central California*, David Alt and Donald Hyndman say of the coast's underlying structure, "The Franciscan complex is one of the world's grand messes."

Doris Sloan, a geologist at the University of California, Berkeley, has a kindlier take on coastal California. "Exasperating," she says, "but exciting." Geologists like rock formations that tell a story. In the Franciscan Complex, Sloan says, the story has been difficult to decipher.

Mel Erskine, who calls himself a "big picture" sort of geologist and is active with the Northern California Geological Society, says, "The mélange," meaning the Franciscan Complex, "contains a great mixture of rock types, some of them quite large. The mélange has blocks in it that are several miles long and several hundred feet thick, all the way down to fist-sized rocks."

On Arlington Avenue in El Cerrito, geologist Ron Crane puts his knife blade to a rock that is dearly loved by its owner, Don Tieck, who has topped it with a lighthouse. "Graywacke," Crane says, identifying one of the most common rocks of the Franciscan Complex, a kind of sandstone. "It's one of the rocks geologists hate. There's nothing nice about them. They're just a mess."

The Franciscan Complex, which forms much of the Berkeley Hills, does offer geologists their share of thrills, however. Often found here, for example, is blueschist, a marvelous, easily shattered, grayish rock that often crops out in immense exposures and takes on a blue gleam in sunlight.

Rare almost everywhere else, blueschist is common here because of the peculiar way California

In the Franciscan Complex, the story has been difficult to decipher.

A dominant geological feature of the Berkeley Hills is the north-south aligned Hayward Fault, the result of northward movement of the tectonic plate on the western side of the hills.

was formed—through subduction. As the Pacific Plate slid beneath the North American Plate, plastering deposits of rock and muck onto the western edge of the continent, the peculiar combination of high pressure and low temperature created the metamorphic rock known as schist.

"Congratulations on your blueschist," Crane tells homeowner John Fornoff. "Geologists come from all around the world to see this," Crane says, adding, "In the Bay Area you can find it almost everyplace, in every park."

It wasn't subduction alone that assembled the Berkeley Hills and their rocks. The same forces that created California immediately set about crumpling, jumbling, heating, and transforming it, while also hauling large portions of it northward, including the rocks in the Berkeley Hills.

"The zone is dynamically active," Mel Erskine says. "So at the same time this material is being plastered onto the continent, it's being sliced up by San Andreas type of motion."

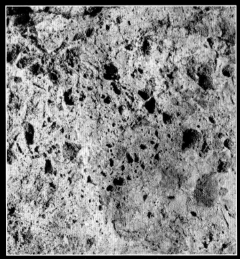

Northbrae rhyolite from Great Stoneface Park.

Blueschist from Murieta Rock.

Rhyolite tuff from Sibley Regional Preserve.

As the plates moved against each other, the forces they generated created the Sierra Nevada and, much later, the coastal ranges. Rocks that began as simple sediments were cooked and transformed, or metamorphosed, and structures that were once horizontal are now vertical or twisted into curves.

The landforms of northern and central California changed radically some 10 to 15 million years ago, when many species of mammals were taking on their present appearance. Tectonic forces were creating a series of volcanoes that have given the Berkeley Hills their beloved Northbrae rhyolite. These are the slate gray and cream-colored rocks, often with a rust-colored tinge and lime green patches of moss and lichens, that climbers enjoy at Indian Rock and Mortar Rock parks. They also pop up through many backyards and basements in Thousand Oaks, giving the neighborhood the look of a giant volcanic field.

San Franciscan chert, the sedimentary rock that underlies the Berkeley Hills.

Leona rhyolite.

Flow banding in rhyolite.

The Northbrae rhyolite boulders differ from rocks in nearby areas in both their age and their geochemistry, says geologist Lin Murphy, who has studied them closely. "These rocks were very probably erupted somewhere to the south, and pieces of them transported north within the fault zone to their present location," she says. "What makes them seem to pop up in this very limited area is an unanswered question."

Many people think they're granite, but they're not. Like granite, rhyolite is produced from magma and is light gray because of its high silica content. But unlike granite, which forms as a flow of magma deep underground and cools very slowly, usually over countless years, rhyolite forms from a surface eruption. Granite has time to form crystals as it cools. Rhyolite, on the other hand, often cools so quickly that it takes on a glassy texture with small crystals that are generally hard to see. Its cooling layers, however, can be clearly seen—especially if a geologist like Ron Crane is there to point them out.

Structures that were once horizontal are now vertical or twisted into curves.

Unlike basalt, which gushes from a volcanic center like oil, rhyolite flows like molasses, Crane says. Thick and viscous, it cools more quickly than it flows. He points out flow banding, which is clearly visible in the boulders at Indian Rock Park and Great Stoneface Park. The bands range from less than an inch to several inches thick, and each represents one flow of lava, which was soon covered by another, then another.

"It's the same thing as putting chocolate syrup over ice cream," he says. "You see the same effects." For a delicious geology lesson, you can try it at home: "Let it pour, then stop, let it pour, then stop. You'll see little wave fronts solidifying, and then you'll have something much like rhyolite."

Crane can see much more in these rocks, of course. He points out where the rock fractured

In Sibley Regional Preserve, the once-horizontal strata of tuff breccia that filled much of the original volcano's caldera is now tilted and folded.

even as it solidified and other fractures caused by the infiltration of water. The reddish marks are a form of rust and indicate iron oxides. The yellowish brown markings indicate limonite, another form of iron oxides. The green comes from lichens and mosses.

In Thousand Oaks, many people believe the neighborhood is sitting on a single gigantic rock. "I think of it as the Thousand Oaks rock," says Kathy Hoare, who has rocks on all sides of her house, "and every one of these houses has an element of the Thousand Oaks rock, under the house or in the backyard, or going through the garage or in the basement, or serving as the driveway."

"We're on a mountain … what you're seeing is only the tip of the rock."

Maybe yes, maybe no, according to Crane. Widely dispersed surface outcroppings may join up below, but they might not. And it's difficult to say how deep the outcrops penetrate. What is true, however, is what Kathy's husband, Tyler, suggests: "We're on a mountain. You can call it a rock, but what you're seeing is only the tip of the rock."

Volcanic they may be, but it's not clear exactly what volcanic eruption produced the rocks of the Thousand Oaks volcanic field. Sibley, most geologists say, referring to the remains of a volcanic cone splayed open on its side for any rock hound to tour at the Robert Sibley Volcanic Regional Preserve. Sibley was part of a family of volcanoes that blew between 12 and 8 million years ago. One of those cones, perhaps the biggest, is now concealed beneath Lawrence Berkeley National Laboratory in the hills behind the university campus.

Several geologists, however, believe that the source was a separate volcanic event that occurred hundreds of miles to the south, near present-day Hollister. One of these is Lin Murphy, who worked with U.S. Geological Survey scientists to date the Northbrae rhyolite at Indian Rock. She believes

The Robert Sibley Volcanic Regional Preserve in the Oakland Hills features volcanic formations from 10 million years ago. The pit is the site of an old quarry from which massive amounts of basalt lava were removed. The largest remaining volcano is Roundtop, which slopes up to the left. Modern park visitors have created a labyrinth at the bottom of the pit—one of several labyrinths in the park.

A ROCK RAISES QUESTIONS IN THE FLATLANDS

The fortresslike rock that supports Albin Renauer and Mary Randolph's house on Sierra Street must weigh several tons—and that's just the part visible to the eye. Still, Renauer says, "I've overheard people walking by saying, 'You think they brought this in?' Get real, man!"

The question is not as absurd as it sounds, however. Renauer and Randolph's home isn't in the Berkeley Hills, where rocks are strewn everywhere, but in the flatlands—or something like the flatlands—and the rock stands out like a visitor from another planet. Many flatlanders never get to the hills, so they aren't ready for the Renauer-Randolph rock.

Even in the hills, however, it would stand out as something different, because this rock is chert, a fragment of the Franciscan Complex shoved onto the continent up to 115 million years ago after being produced millions of years earlier from layer after layer of microscopic sea creatures. "It just rode in on the oceanic plate," geologist Ron Crane says, "got picked up and carried."

Why is this one of the few rocks in its neighborhood? Because the land it occupies isn't flatlands proper, but a long arm of chert extending from the Berkeley Hills and ending in Renauer and Randolph's front yard, Crane suggests. "This is a little tongue that juts out from the hills," Renauer says. "We're the knob at the end of the swale."

In any case, it's a lovely rock, showing its colors best at dusk—oranges, greens, dark reds. The rock is almost pure quartz, Crane says, thanks to metamorphosis brought on by high temperature and pressure at a time when the rock was at depth within the earth. The formerly horizontal sedimentary layers of dead sea creatures are vertical today, shoved up by tectonic forces. At times they resemble zebra stripes.

Northbrae rhyolite is older than the volcanic rocks at Sibley. The dispute illustrates just how fluid the study of Bay Area geology can be—and how much remains to be discovered.

Murphy, who was once an attorney, developed an interest in rocks by climbing them. Then curiosity took hold, so she got a degree in geology. Why, she wondered, are the East Bay's two types of rhyolite so very different? In addition to the Northbrae rhyolite, there are also outcrops of Leona rhyolite, both named early in the twentieth century after the neighborhoods in which they are found. At that time they were thought to be of similar age and origin.

"As a climber, it didn't seem to me that the Northbrae rhyolite was like the Leona rhyolite, because the Leona rhyolite is crumbly and fractured. A climber would never try to climb on it because it isn't strong enough to support a climber's weight," Murphy says.

Working with the U.S. Geological Survey, Murphy submitted rock samples to zircon geochronology, a labor-intensive process for dating rocks, and determined that Northbrae rhyolite is much younger than Leona, roughly 11.5 million years old versus 155 million. Her conclusion? The Leona rocks were created by volcanoes long ago and far away, then shoved onto the continent along with the rest of the Franciscan Complex. She believes that the Northbrae came from a much later eruption, but not from Sibley.

Leona rhyolite can be found to the south of the Northbrae outcrops along Tunnel Road in Berkeley and, to the north, in Alvarado Park in Richmond, which is part of Wildcat Canyon Regional Park. Although its volcanic origins are clear enough, Leona rhyolite is hard to read because it's had a long, hard life.

Thundereggs are spherical nodules usually a few inches in diameter that form in some types of silica-rich rocks like rhyolite. Thundereggs got their popular name from Native Americans but they are also known as lithophysae (Latin for "rock bubbles"). Samples have been collected from Northbrae rhyolite on Spruce Street in North Berkeley. When these nodules are cut open, they reveal a hollow, star-shaped cavity.

Thundereggs form as molten lava cools and steam and other gases are trapped in bubbles. Silica minerals often crystallize around these bubbles. "Later, silica-rich solutions may enter the cavity and fill it with banded agate, chalcedony, clear quartz crystals, or even amethyst," writes geologist Richard Carwell.

Opposite: Mortar Rock Park.

Whether Northbrae rhyolite arose in the Sibley cones or in some other volcanic family, it's likely that the eruption didn't occur at the latitude or longitude where the cones can be found today. And the Berkeley Rocks were far from Berkeley when they first appeared.

"What often catches people's interest is that the rock wasn't formed here," says Erskine. "It was formed down by Hayward, or down by Hollister. And it's been moving ever since." The rocks have been carried along by the movement of the Hayward Fault.

Rocks created by the same volcanic eruptions can be found elsewhere in the Bay Area, Erskine says, including Mount Burdell in Marin County and the Quien Sabe volcanic rocks near Hollister.

The Berkeley Hills have many other forms of rock, including several whose genesis is unclear. Pinnacle Rock in Remillard Park and Founders' Rock at the university "probably originated as part of ocean crust and have been much altered by hot fluids in the fault zone," Murphy says.

Indian Rock by night.

Graywacke, a sedimentary rock in which individual grains of sand can be spotted, is everywhere. Soft and easy to work, it's often found in the decorative columns that dot the region's neighborhoods. Chert, another sedimentary rock, can also be found. Often formed by layer after layer of dead single-cell marine animals, chert shows bands of white, black, and green and breaks easily into chunks.

Cragmont Rock, a popular climbing spot, is what Crane calls an "agglomerate." Using a tiny hand lens, he identifies pebbles and gravel worn down from rhyolite boulders, other chunks of rock, and volcanic glass. But no lens is needed to see the expanses of volcanic ash, chalk white and crumbly to the touch. Some of the better cemented ash, which may have come from the same eruptions that produced the rhyolite flows, has been used to construct the stone building at the base of Cragmont Rock.

Geologist Walter Alvarez, who won fame for postulating that collision of an asteroid or comet with the earth resulted in the extinction of the dinosaurs, also won popularity in his Thousand Oaks neighborhood when he argued some decades back that Picnic Rock should be spared from development.

"In a gently molded landscape like ours, where real bedrock is almost everywhere hidden by a mantle of soft, decayed rock and ancient landslide debris, the few outcrops of bedrock are especially precious," he wrote. "They provide an element of surprise and contrast in the landscape. And they remind us that the Berkeley Hills are not just the rounded piles of dirt they appear to be, but that they have an intricate internal structure that can tell us the history of this part of the earth back through millions of years."

The Berkeley rocks were far from Berkeley when they first appeared.

II. EARLY INHABITANTS

THE NATIVE AMERICANS WHO LIVED in the East Bay before the arrival of Spanish missionaries would have a hard time recognizing their old neighborhoods today. The shoreline has been extended into the Bay, and seasonal marshes have been covered with homes. Rolling grasslands dotted with oaks have suffered the same fate, and hillsides that were largely barren of trees have been urbanized and forested.

But the rocks remain.

Back in 1911, a Berkeley newspaper wondered, "Did Indians Dwell Where the Parks Are?" The *Independent* was referring to Thousand Oaks, Northbrae, and Cragmont, which were being carved into home sites by developers who encouraged the public—would-be home buyers, all—to visit and picnic.

The answer, of course, is yes. But both question and answer still give historians pause. In the century and a half since urbanization hit the East Bay, most evidence of Indian settlement—shell mounds, mortar holes carved into rocks, designs carved into rocks—has been demolished, scattered, stolen, or defaced.

Some of the earliest petroglyphs, or carvings, made in rocks by the first humans to frequent the Bay Area were small cups and grooves. Larger holes were used for grinding acorns.

That's why asking those in the know about settlements in the hills produces hemming and haw-ing and justifiable warnings. Archeological sites contain almost the only information about what the Bay Area's original inhabitants ate, how they dressed, what tools they used, and how their culture changed over the centuries.

"Public knowledge of these sites leads to their destruction," says Richard Schwartz, author of the book *Berkeley 1900*, who has made studying Indian settlements his avocation. "It was a very var-ied and rich culture. We owe it to them, and to the future, to protect these sites."

Early in the twentieth century, an anthropologist counted more than four hundred shell mounds—piles of discarded shells, tools, and other debris from civilization—around San Francisco Bay and its hinterlands. By midcentury, N.C. Nelson reported, most had been obliterated, covered up by houses and roads, their materials scattered. "It is said that the mound material, mixed with rock salt, produces tennis courts that for combined firmness and elasticity, are unexcelled," he wrote.

Some rocks served as canvases for Indian rock art.

The Ohlone Indians gathered shellfish along the Bay and acorns beneath the oaks that dotted the flatlands and hills. Many rocks in the Berkeley Hills have deep mortar holes, often four or five inches in diameter on top and six or more inches deep. These were used for grinding acorns, a staple of the Ohlone diet. Some rocks in the East Bay hills even served as canvases for Indian rock art. These petroglyphs—images and symbols carved into rocks—are up to 8,000 years old.

" … things like prominent rocks had histories and geneses … They were there for a purpose."

While most archeological evidence of Ohlone Indian acorn grinding is in the mortar holes on some of the larger Berkeley-area boulders, occasionally other examples come to light. This mortar and pestle were found near a massive boulder during a remodeling project on Vincente Avenue.

Since the East Bay's Ohlone Indians were moved onto missions at the start of the 1800s, much of what we know about their way of life is speculative and based on what we know about Indian life elsewhere in the state, says Malcolm Margolin, whose 1978 book *The Ohlone Way* spurred on further researchers. "Throughout California, things like prominent rocks had histories and geneses," he says. "They were there for a purpose. They tended to be sacred. They tended to have life and power if you went there. This was true throughout California, and we assume it was true for Berkeley. But the particulars have been lost."

Still, the mortar holes that have been discovered at Mortar Rock Park, and in many other rocks throughout the hills, show that Ohlone people gathered at the rocks for their daily tasks. That suggests they lived nearby.

Additionally, Ohlone tools have been found near Berkeley's rocks. Michael Cohn and Molly Stone, the owners of a wonderful rock in Thousand Oaks, perhaps the largest freestanding chunk of rhyolite hidden in a private backyard, discovered intact rock artifacts beneath their basement, including portable mortars and pestles, scraping tools, and hammers.

California's Indians used rocks as axes, drills, hammers, arrow straighteners, and jewelry, as well as for ceremonial purposes. What anthropologists call "charmstones," pendantlike objects of greenstone, chert, serpentinite, schist, or graywacke, have been found buried with their owners. Stones were also used for cooking; these early inhabitants heated stones in a fire, then tossed them into baskets to cook acorn mush.

The Indians had a very good understanding of the qualities of different rock types and selected

PETROGLYPHS

The marks made by the Ohlone in the rhyolite and blueschist rocks characteristic of the Berkeley Hills had both functional and religious significance, and can still be found in the parks along Baxter Creek in El Cerrito. Radio carbon dating of shell mounds believed to be from the same period suggests 4,000 years of Ohlone habitation in the East Bay, but Bay Area Rock Art Association expert Leigh Marymor suggests the petroglyphs in Baxter Creek are much older. "Capules and other features on the stone lead us to believe that this site may have been in use for 5,000 to 8,000 years," Marymor writes, referring to the boulder in Canyon Trails Park.

The Ohlone used the nearby creek water to leach the tannins from the acorns they ground into a paste on the massive rocks surrounding the creek. In addition to the mortar-grinding holes, the boulders have scores of cuplike depressions with grooves incised along their sides that suggest some ceremonial or ritual use of the site. What the markings represent is the subject of speculation. According to Marymor, similar cup-and-groove petroglyph boulders, frequented by the Pomo

people of California's Mendocino and Lake counties, were associated with fertility rituals and known locally as "baby rocks." These "pecked" oval or circular forms—referred to by archeologists as the "pecked curvilinear nucleated" (PNC) petroglyph style—are concentrated in the northern Bay Area, but have been found from the Oregon border to Santa Barbara and in the North and Central Coast mountain ranges.

For more than forty years, the rock at Baxter Creek was part of a sandbox and children's playground that featured a wooden canoe and teepee, and it suffered abrasion as it was explored by kids with sandy shoes. Today the boulders of Baxter Creek are the centerpiece of a wild "cultural landscape garden," complete with ponds and native grasses, and they are not identified in any way so as to minimize the likelihood of their being defaced. To the untrained eye they look like just a few more of the boulders that dot the creeks and valleys of the East Bay hills.

specific rocks for various purposes. Steatite, a form of soapstone, was carved into tobacco pipes because it doesn't break when heated. Basalt was used for mortars because it's strong. Obsidian made good arrowheads.

Many Indian quarries have been found throughout the state. They appear to have been communally owned. Stones were often traded over long distances, but most were used within 150 miles of where they were quarried.

The Thousand Oaks area was known as the "Indian Burial Grounds" early in the twentieth century, when it was in the news daily. Efforts to turn the area into an immense regional park failed when voters said no in 1907.

In 1911, the *Independent* reported that, beneath what is now a street in Thousand Oaks, scientists had discovered a shell mound that marked a large village. "Here was the headquarters of the chiefs of the tribes," their reporter wrote, and daydreamed: "It is easy to imagine that the news of the appearance of the early Spanish galleons was flashed from this rock to the scattered bands all about the bay."

Indian Trail, one of hundreds of paths linking the streets that follow the contours of the Berkeley Hills, may have been an Ohlone trail once. It runs downhill from Yosemite Avenue and Great Stoneface Park to The Alameda. This area was known as the Indian Burial Grounds during the development of Thousand Oaks in the early 1900s.

THE ROCKS DURING THE SPANISH AND MEXICAN ERAS

For decades after the East Bay was settled by Spain, the Berkeley Hills remained undeveloped, devoted almost entirely to cattle grazing. The impressive outcroppings of rhyolite, schist, and serpentinite remained in plain view—so much so that one outcropping was used to demarcate the immense rancho that occupied much of the East Bay.

Rancho San Antonio, which was given free and clear to Luis Peralta for his thirty years of military service to Spain, stretched from San Leandro Creek in the south to Albany Hill in the north, 48,000 acres of oak-dotted grassland and chaparral.

On a horseback ride with their father through the property in 1820, two of Peralta's sons, Domingo and Antonio, spotted a picturesque crag high in the hills from their breakfast spot in the

Rancho San Antonio, located between San Leandro and Cerrito creeks, once stretched from the crest of the hill to the water. The star marks Monument Rock, which is labeled on the map, "Large Rock, rising in the form of a monument, looking to the North."

Pinnacle Rock was once a prominent feature in the hills, as evidenced by this Carleton Watkins photograph. Today it is hidden by houses and massive eucalyptus trees. This twenty-five-foot-tall outcropping of welded tuff (consolidated volcanic ash) is now the centerpiece of Remillard Park, a popular spot among boulderers and picnickers.

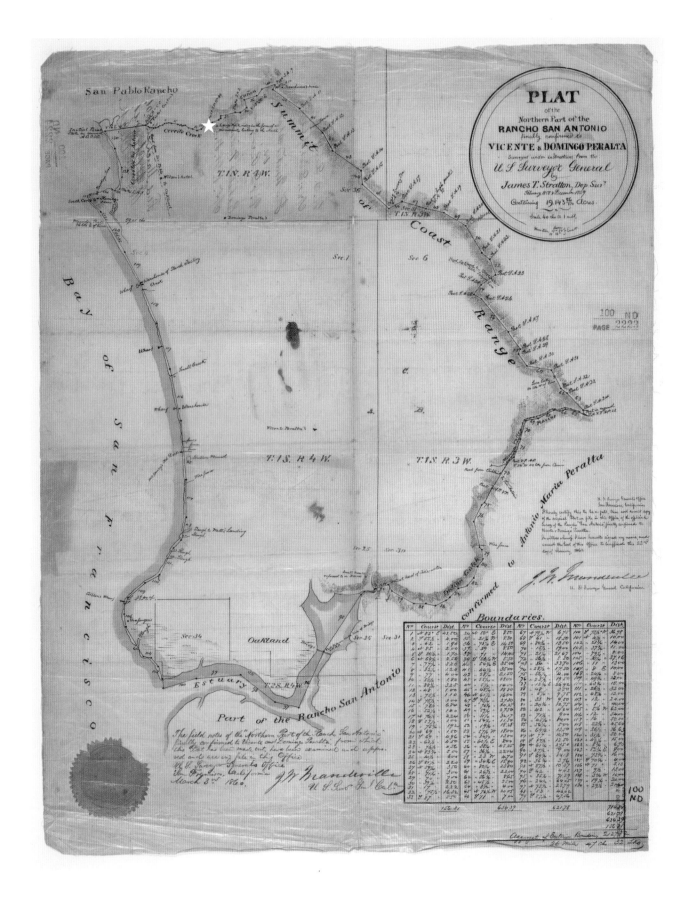

flatlands along Cerrito Creek, the northern boundary of Peralta's ranch. The rock seemed on a line

with the creek, so the Peraltas chose it to mark the northeast corner of their land. The boys climbed

Monument Rock and placed colorful stones within a niche, apparently to mark their ownership of

the land.

Today Monument Rock remains an imposing site, though growth both arboreal and residential

restricts its visibility. A quaint Arts and Crafts bungalow has been built alongside it, and it has been

topped with a deck and a flagpole. From the backyard, however, the rock remains impressive, soar-

ing a good four stories high. The rock's owners, Parviz and C. Ruth Shokat, understand its historical

importance. Parviz, a rock climber, often perches at its summit and reads. The Shokats' relationship

with the rock gets even more intimate at night. They have an open-air sleeping porch built against it,

and that's where they sleep every night.

While trees and a brick and stone cottage
all but obscure this once prominent rock,
Monument Rock continues to be a delight
to its rock climber owners.

MYSTERIOUS WALLS

A series of meandering, at times crudely built low stone walls that wind through the East Bay hills have been the talk of the town for more than a century, ever since Harold French, founder of the Contra Costa Hills Club, discovered them on a ramble.

The walls can be found from Berkeley to San Jose in short sections (the photograph above was taken just off the Seaview Trail in Tilden Park). Fans—who call themselves "wall nuts"—have suggested that if the sections were strung together, they'd stretch twenty miles. They may not be beautiful, but they are mysterious—and that's their charm. No one can say for sure how they got here. But much gets said nonetheless.

"Walls convince scientists that America's first civilization was Mongolian," the *San Francisco Chronicle* reported in 1904, comparing them to the Great Wall of China. "Was Oakland [an] ancient battleground?" the *Oakland Tribune* asked eight years later, accompanying its article with an illustration showing Neanderthals tossing rocks at each other. Others have suggested that the walls are pre-Columbian or were created by Druids—or the Amish. They still attract New Agers, who speak of their power.

Other observers believe they may have been constructed by sheep herders.

III. DEVELOPMENT IN THE BERKELEY HILLS

THE IDEA OF BUILDING IN HARMONY WITH NATURE came to Berkeley early. Just after the university was founded in the 1860s, landscape designer Frederick Law Olmsted designed a neighborhood of curving roadways that would lead elegantly to Oakland, leaving charming home sites in its wake. Olmsted, who had designed New York's Central Park and would go on to design the parks and parkways of Boston, was a man whose visions were in the forefront of planning theory, combining grand classical schemes with naturalistic ambiance. To get a small glimpse of what Olmsted had in mind, explore Piedmont Avenue south of campus and try to picture the area without the traffic. Unfortunately little else of his plan went into effect.

His proposal suggests, however, just how widespread such ideas were in the latter half of the nineteenth century. In England, planned communities were being constructed that blended Beaux-Arts classicism—wide axial boulevards, for example—with narrower, curved lanes that hugged the contours of the land. And in north Berkeley in the 1880s, long before the birth of the Hillside Club, Caspar Hopkins laid out his Peralta Park with curved roadways on the site of Domingo Peralta's old homestead.

One of the urns from the sales motif used by developer John Spring sits at the bottom of Indian Trail on The Alameda.

41

THE HILLSIDE CLUB

The Hillside Club, founded by a group of feisty ladies in the late 1890s, is often credited with setting Berkeley on its course of building with nature. But the club was just one player in that movement. Developers, including Duncan McDuffie and John H. Spring, and engineers, landscape designers, and planners, including Charles Huggins, Mark Daniels, John Gregg, R. E. Mansell, and John Galen Howard, heard the same music and sang a similar tune.

The Hillside women, several of whom were school principals, were influenced by architect Bernard Maybeck and his friend Charles Keeler, whose 1904 book *The Simple Home* derived some of its principles from Maybeck's architecture. A house Maybeck designed for Keeler in 1895, all shingles and open beams and warm redwood, set the tone for Berkeley's rustic brown-shingle look.

The women of the Hillside Club were influenced not so much by what they preferred as by what they abhorred—the ornate Queen Anne Victorian homes that marched in military file up every hillside in San Francisco and had made inroads on Berkeley hillsides as well. "One looks towards God's everlasting hills for rest and peace," club founder Madge Robinson wrote in 1899, "but where can rest and peace be found, so long as our portion of these, God's hills, is scarred with such unhealthy growths, such freaks of houses?"

The club's principles, announced the year before, included "narrow country roads" winding "at an easy grade" and bordered by trees, and irregular lots with houses arranged "in studied groups, to avoid obstruction of a neighbor's views." Wood should be natural, "colored by the weather" and neither painted nor stained—except for window casings, and then only "dull brown." Broad eaves were encouraged, but towers shunned. "A tower, an arch or a round window is essentially indicative

"… but where can rest and peace be found, so long as our portion of these, God's hills, is scarred with such unhealthy growths, such freaks of houses?"

The founder of the Sierra Club, John Muir (right), was a contemporary and acquaintance of Charles Keeler (left).

of stone or brick masonry and is illogical and ugly in wood." Inside, built-in sideboards were encouraged and "factory-made articles" banned.

The women did more than set fashion. They politicked. When a school in the hills was proposed in 1901, they insisted that it be shingled and have open-beamed ceilings—and won. They fought again when the city planned to extend Cedar Street into the hills in a straight line—and lost. So they called on their men, and that made the difference. "The women had no votes in those days," wrote Mrs. Todd, a member of the club, "but their husbands had. That's the reason we have those lovely, winding roads. They are winding all right and they can't be unwound."

In 1902, bowing to political realities, the club invited men to join and agreed that a man would always be president. Maybeck joined, and Keeler served as president until 1905.

DEVELOPING THE HILLS

After the 1906 San Francisco earthquake, Berkeley became a boomtown. The fourth-fastest growing city in the United States, it increased in population from thirteen thousand to more than forty thousand, from midsize town to small city, between 1900 and 1910. That first decade of the twentieth century saw the rise of several real estate developers and speculators who would guide Berkeley's growth in a surprisingly wise manner, among them Duncan McDuffie and John H. Spring.

It was the developers, and the planners and architects they worked with, who really created Berkeley's natural hillside neighborhoods, not the Hillside Club. "The people at that time were inspired," says Paul Grunland, a longtime tour leader with the Berkeley Historical Society. "They wanted to make the world a better place. If they were going to do a development with their names on it, they wanted it to be a good one."

"The people at that time were inspired ... They wanted to make the world a better place."

Their neighborhoods arrayed homes on streets contoured to the natural hillsides and depended on commuter rail to get workers to jobs in San Francisco, Oakland, and Berkeley. To speed pedestrians downhill to streetcar stops, a network of pathways was provided, many of them precipitously steep. Today some are tree-shaded and have a rural feel, and some are surrounded by rocks or accommodate rocks in the middle of the path. The trails remain one of the treasures of the Berkeley Hills.

The rocks played a large role in attracting buyers to the neighborhoods. Advertisements and newspaper "articles" that were advertisements in disguise often included photos of the rocks. Some developers went a step further. "In anticipation of the grand opening of the North Cragmont tract,

The Marin Circle fountain, circa 1912.

(continued on page 51)

"HIGH-CLASS HOMES FOR CULTURED PEOPLE"

To market the new neighborhoods of north Berkeley in the boom years of the early twentieth century, developers and real estate agents arranged picnic tours of the rock- and oak-studded hillsides for potential buyers. They also published lavish flyers, ads, and brochures extolling the neighborhoods' superior climate and scenery, the elegance and taste of the developments' planning, and the convenience and exclusivity of life there.

Examples range from this ardent catalog of Thousand Oaks' horticultural improvements (from a sales pamphlet):

To give you an idea of the arboreal and floral beauties of the grounds, we mention these important facts: One thousand double red hawthornes line the winding oil macadam roads, paralleled with terraces in which are laid 40,000 geraniums and gazenias [sic]; rows of Lombardy poplars set as walls excluding adjacent sections; yellow blooming broom plants, the red flowering eucalyptus, azaleas, dwarf maples, creeping juniper, liquid amber [sic], red oak and Italian cypress trees adorn the hillsides. All these features are but a few of the many artificial additions to the exceptional, natural beauties of this exclusive residence site.

to this oddly insistent paean to Berkeley's fine climate (from an ad in *Sunset* magazine appar-

ently aimed at people from the central and eastern parts of the country):

You get a free prize package of climate with every square foot of land that you acquire in Berkeley, whether by purchase, lease or rent. This is a generous gift of Nature, of which no one can deprive you. Day by day you breathe it in. You cannot sell it or give it away. It is a delightful premium that goes with and is part of the joy of living in Berkeley.

Allowing for changing styles in copywriting, these marketing pieces from a century ago still capture some of the reasons these neighborhoods remain cherished places to live.

Entrance Vista, "Thousand Oaks"

Above: A page from a promotional booklet depicts one of the massive concrete urns that were the marketing motif for the Thousand Oaks development. Right: The front and back covers of a Mason-McDuffie brochure for Northbrae. Opposite: (above) The cover of the booklet, "The Story of a Berkeley Home," and (below) a real estate agent's promotional postcard depicting a stretch of Arlington Avenue.

DUNCAN MCDUFFIE, DEVELOPER AND ENVIRONMENTALIST

Duncan McDuffie (1877–1951) told friends he worked for one reason—so he could afford to vacation in the Sierras "sniffing the trees." An early leader of the Sierra Club, McDuffie hiked as often as he could and pioneered several routes, including portions of today's Pacific Crest Trail. McDuffie helped create the East Bay Regional Park District and helped found the State Park Council, which established the state park system.

But he was also a canny developer who turned vast tracts of the Berkeley Hills into some of the Bay Area's best-loved suburbs. McDuffie, who loved gardening as much as

mountaineering, insisted that his streets, which he called "pleasure drives," be curved and lined with trees.

McDuffie hired the engineer Charles Huggins to lay out some of his neighborhoods and brought in John Galen Howard, the architect who oversaw the planning and design of the Berkeley campus of the University of California, to create entry gates of local stone. Howard also created the wonderful fountain in the center of the Arlington Circle, topped with whimsical statues of bears by sculptor Arthur Putnam.

Above: The San Antonio Home Owners Association has a glorious communal grove of oaks shading large rhyolite boulders, a swimming pool, and a wonderful fieldstone fireplace, all well hidden from the road now. These grounds were once part of the John Hopkins Spring Estate at San Antonio and the Arlington.

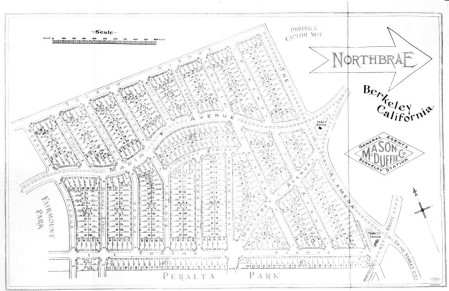

Left: Mason McDuffie's first development in north Berkeley— the Northbrae tract flanking Marin Avenue west of The Alameda.

Right: John Spring's mansion was modeled on the Empress Elisabeth of Austria's palace on the Greek island of Corfu. Designed by John Hudson Thomas, the two-story Beaux-Arts-influenced house was built entirely of concrete. The house and two other buildings on the original estate were designated a City of Berkeley Landmark in 2000.

JOHN SPRING, DEVELOPER AND GAMBLER

John H. Spring, who developed Thousand Oaks in the 1910s, went through many ups and downs in his life but never lost his willingness to gamble. Spring married one fortune in the 1880s and inherited another, speculated in real estate, owned a quarry in Berkeley and a gold mine in Calaveras County, and partnered in several real estate developments. One story says he lost control of the Claremont Hotel in a game of dominos.

Spring, who profited mightily from the San Francisco earthquake, once owned most of Albany. He built a mansion in Thousand Oaks—still one of the largest houses in Berkeley—in an effort to promote the neighborhood. "He erected the great house of reinforced concrete at the time of his lowest ebb financially—when he owed more than a million dollars, and was land poor," columnist Hal Johnson wrote in the *Berkeley Daily Gazette*. "He had sold thousands of dollars worth of home sites in that vicinity on the strength that he would build his own home there. And he kept faith with buyers."

The mansion, adorned with steps and a fireplace of the local stone, opened onto one of Berkeley's grandest rock parks, a rhyolite-strewn hillside shaded by live oaks. The house was designed in 1912 by John Hudson Thomas.

Spring was associated with Duncan McDuffie in several developments, and followed principles similar to McDuffie's in laying out Thousand Oaks. When Spring died at age seventy-one in 1933, the papers said his greatest monument was the Spring Mansion. But that's not true. It's Thousand Oaks itself.

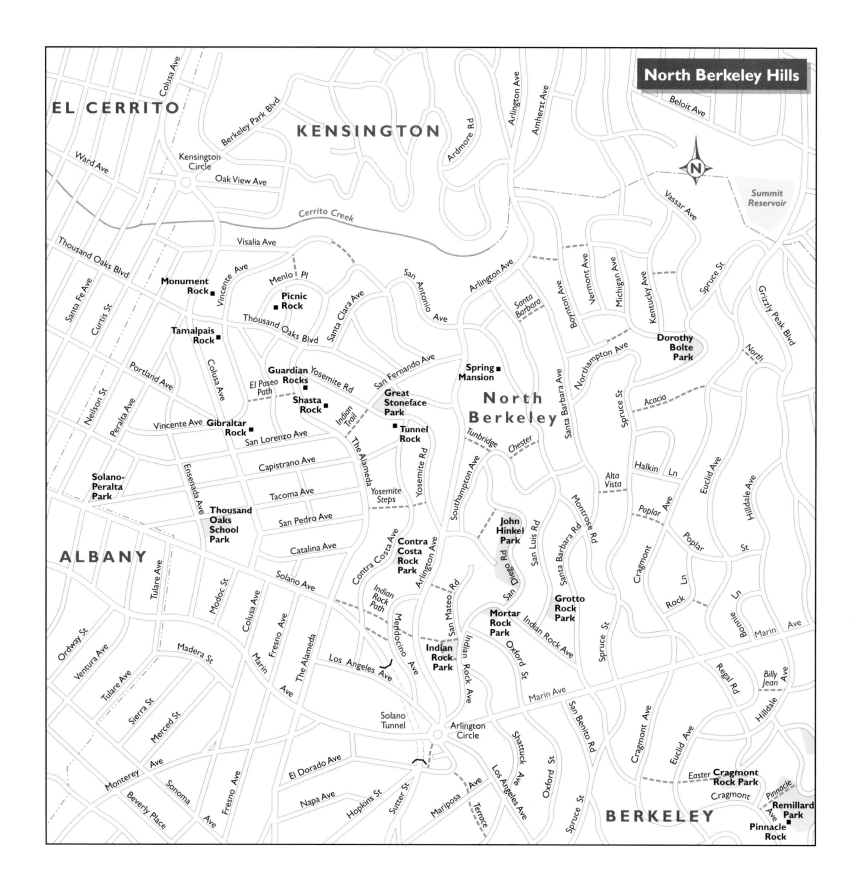

the rocky promontory that stands as a silent sentinel over the peaceful slope has been painted white and can be seen in San Francisco," the *Berkeley Daily Gazette* announced in 1908, adding, "The white sentry will be the lodestone that will draw thousands to the attractive spot tomorrow."

Northbrae, Claremont, and Thousand Oaks

Among the men who ensured that boomtown Berkeley maintained its bucolic air were McDuffie, of the Mason-McDuffie firm, which developed the Northbrae and Claremont subdivisions; Spring, who developed Thousand Oaks; and the landscape designers and architects R. E. Mansell, John Gregg, and John Galen Howard.

These were the men Mark Daniels had in mind when he wrote about "those who make a business of turning natural beauty to practical ends in forming home sites for persons of refined taste."

McDuffie and Spring allied with streetcar companies to provide service to their subdivisions and promoted the new neighborhoods with purple prose. Spring's associate Daniels, a landscape engineer, architect, and journalist, emerged as a leading booster for the new neighborhoods of the East Bay.

The rocks played a large role in attracting buyers to the neighborhoods.

"What finer setting for childhood's development, for instilling only ideas of beauty, and appreciation of Nature's bountifulness than this sylvan scene—a California wooded hillside turned into a place of homes," he wrote in *California Magazine*. The scene he described shows a young girl climbing a set of stone steps toward a large rock, perhaps the rock in front of his own Thousand Oaks home.

"The more beautiful we make our homes," Daniels continued, "the more beautiful will be our lives, the more wholesome our outlook upon the world, and the less apt will we be to allow our minds to become possessed of unhallowed thoughts."

"Delicate piece of landscape engineering," reads the caption of one photo in Daniels's article, "fitting a road between two enormous boulders."

Neighborhoods by McDuffie and Spring take advantage of the local rock by incorporating it into architectural features. Entry pillars that mark prominent intersections (hallmarks of some of McDuffie's developments) are made of the local stone, as are occasional entry gates and commuter rail stops, including those at the Uplands entry to Claremont. The rocks were also incorporated into many homes as foundations, basement walls, chimneys, and occasional facades.

The pillars of local stone bearing street names are included in the broad designation of the Northbrae Public Improvements as a City of Berkeley Landmark. The "public improvements" were designed by John Galen Howard as part of R. E. Mansell's 1907 overall landscape plan for roads and paths. There are some thirty pillars in Northbrae (more in Cragmont). The entrance to the estate was marked by two larger pillars on The Alameda where the North Berkeley Public Library now stands.

Northbrae, Claremont, and Thousand Oaks were "restricted residence parks," with rules governing the size, cost, and appearance of homes, forbidding business or industry, and restricting racial minorities. The developers sold lots and either built homes for the buyers or suggested architects.

Berkeley the State Capital?

Arlington Circle wasn't designed merely to entice home buyers. Developers Louis Titus and Duncan McDuffie hoped to convince the state to move the capital from Sacramento to Berkeley by donating forty choice acres. They named streets in the neighborhood after California counties: Mendocino, Napa, Los Angeles, Fresno, Monterey, and Colusa.

The "capital removal" effort was in full swing by 1907. McDuffie trumpeted the notion in his advertising: "Berkeley! The future capital of California! The educational capital of the Pacific Coast! The fastest growing city on San Francisco Bay!"

The Berkeley Chamber of Commerce backed the plan, as did the city itself and the University of California. Many state workers did, too. Sacramento was a remote town in those days, so to get their business done bureaucrats often had to travel to San Francisco.

"Legislators Pleased by the Site," the *Berkeley Reporter* headlined in February 1907. "Balboa and his party could not have felt greater pride as they stood upon the crest of a lofty ridge and looked for the first time upon the Pacific than did the local committee of the Chamber of Commerce Saturday afternoon when, with nearly two hundred legislators, their wives and attachés, they stood upon the rolling plateau," the article continued.

The capitol buildings would have been sited at the southeast corner of Solano Avenue and The Alameda. A proposed regional park would have been directly behind the capitol.

Backers of the plan convinced the state legislature to place it on the ballot. But opponents argued that legislation needs lubrication—and Berkeley was a dry town (officially, at least). Others said the effort was more about marketing real estate than improving state governance.

By the time the plan came to a vote in November 1908, even local supporters knew it would fail. Coverage of the vote was muted, overshadowed by the presidential race between William Howard Taft and William Jennings Bryan. Only three counties supported "capital removal": San Francisco, Alameda, and Santa Clara. "Berkeley stood up loyally on the capital removal bill and cast a good majority," the *Berkeley Daily Gazette* reported. "The campaign has advertised Berkeley throughout the state and is worth 10 times the cost even if the bill does not carry. It proves that Berkeley is alive and active and doing things."

Turning Thousand Oaks into a Public Park

The effort to turn Berkeley into the state capital may have seemed a long shot, even to its supporters. Not so, however, the attempt to turn most of what is today called Thousand Oaks into a regional park. No one reading through old copies of the *Berkeley Daily Gazette* as election day neared can avoid rooting for the efforts of Mrs. Elinore Carlisle, W. J. Mortimer, and the rest of the city's "progressive elements" to create what former San Francisco mayor James Phelan proclaimed "a park that is already made."

If the measure had passed, Thousand Oaks would today be nothing but trees, trails—and rocks!

The park would have stretched roughly from Peralta Avenue east almost to Arlington, and from Cerrito Creek—the county line—south almost to Solano Avenue. Although neither Indian Rock

Pedestrian walkway over the Solano Tunnel near Arlington Circle.

nor Mortar Rock would have been in the park, it would have included many of the largest rocks in the Northbrae volcanic field, including Monument Rock, Picnic Rock, Contra Costa Rock, and others equally imposing although unnamed. Almost every photo that ran in the *Gazette* about the proposed park focused on individual rocks or rock-strewn fields.

The plan before the people was simple—spend $980,000 for the 980 acres known as the "Indian Burial Grounds."

Proponents, led by the Chamber of Commerce, argued that the city needed "breathing space," and that "Berkeley is the fourth city in size in California and yet it doesn't have a park to its name." Opponents, whom the far-from-neutral *Gazette* identified as "the ultra-conservative element, which invariably asserts itself in Berkeley affairs," complained that the land was outside the city limits and too expensive. Duncan McDuffie urged voters to approve the purchase, calling it "a ridiculously low price."

"Until one has visited this beautiful body of land one cannot appreciate its natural advantages and attractions, and it is safe to predict that it will not long remain on the market for the price of $1,000 an acre," W. J. Mortimer said. "It will be snapped up by private enterprise and retailed in villa sites and investors will be only too glad to pay double or treble the price now asked."

"We should not allow that tract of land that was shaped by the hand of the Almighty to go to waste and be devastated by the hand of man," University of California president Benjamin Ide Wheeler argued.

The battle was hard fought. The chamber offered anyone who wished to visit the site free tickets on the electric railway. "Seldom in its history," the *Gazette* said, "has the city of Berkeley been so aroused over a municipal election."

On election day, 1,702 Berkeley voters backed the park, a majority. But 1,143 did not, and the measure required two-thirds approval. The *Gazette* reported "a feeling of depression" and said of opponents, "Every man jack of them will live to regret it."

Designed by John Galen Howard to be the grand entrance to the proposed state capital, the Beaux-Arts-influenced Marin Circle and Fountain was dedicated in 1911. For decades rail commuters walked up the Fountain Path to their homes in Northbrae from the train depot just below on Henry Street. In 1958 a runaway truck demolished the fountain; it took nearly forty years and donations from 1,200 "Friends of the Fountain and Walk" to create a precise replica of the monument. The original fountain's bear cubs symbolizing the state of California were sculpted by Arthur Putnam; Sarita White sculpted the cubs when the statue was rebuilt. The Marin Circle and Fountain is part of Berkeley Landmark 174.

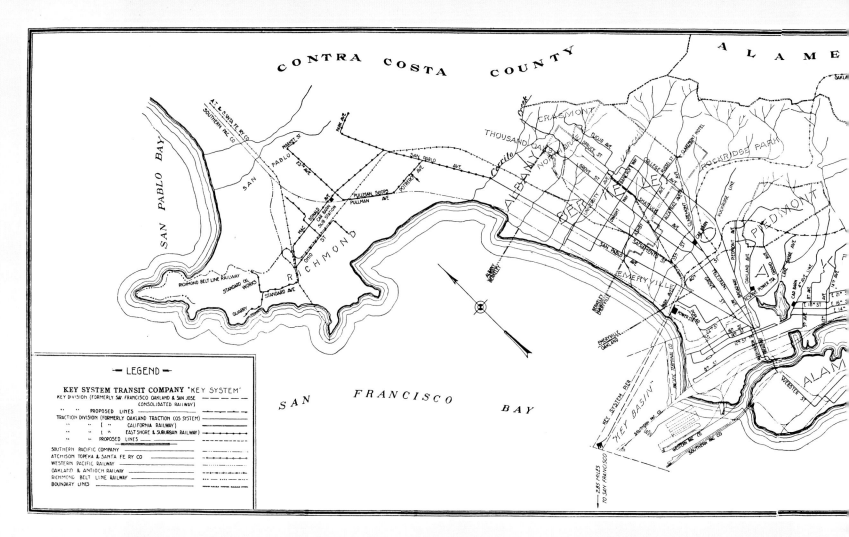

TRAINS IN BERKELEY

The railroad surge of the 1850s and 1860s transformed Rancho Peralta from pasture to cultivated farmland. The area's subsequent urbanization was the result of the extension of trains and streetcar lines into north Berkeley, which made development in the Berkeley Hills feasible. The initial train line built in 1876, a branch line of the Southern Pacific steam powered rail network, ran from Oakland to Berkeley and focused development on what is now Shattuck Square. The line was extended to the Berryman Station depot at Vine Street in 1878, and in 1891 electric rail systems debuted in the Bay Area with a line from

Oakland running up Grove Street (present-day Martin Luther King Jr. Way) to downtown Berkeley. The integrated network of interurban lines that evolved came to be known as the Key System (see map above). These trains whisked commuters to fast propeller-driven ferries that took them to San Francisco. The development of the hills progressed hand in hand with the streetcar lines because both were owned by the same men: Francis Borax Smith and various associates, including Frank Havens and John Spring. They bought land and developed thousands of acres of East Bay residential properties, including large

portions of the Claremont, Northbrae, and Thousand Oaks neighborhoods.

Competition from the Key System forced Southern Pacific to electrify its branch line; the company also extended its electric line along Henry Street to Solano Avenue through the Northbrae Tunnel (built in 1910), which served the Sutter Avenue Rail Station. After 1941, the tunnel was used by the Key System for its F line trains, which ran until 1958. (The tunnel was converted to car use in 1963.) Both businesses developed their own network of streetcar feeder lines that facilitated the commute for residents of north Berkeley

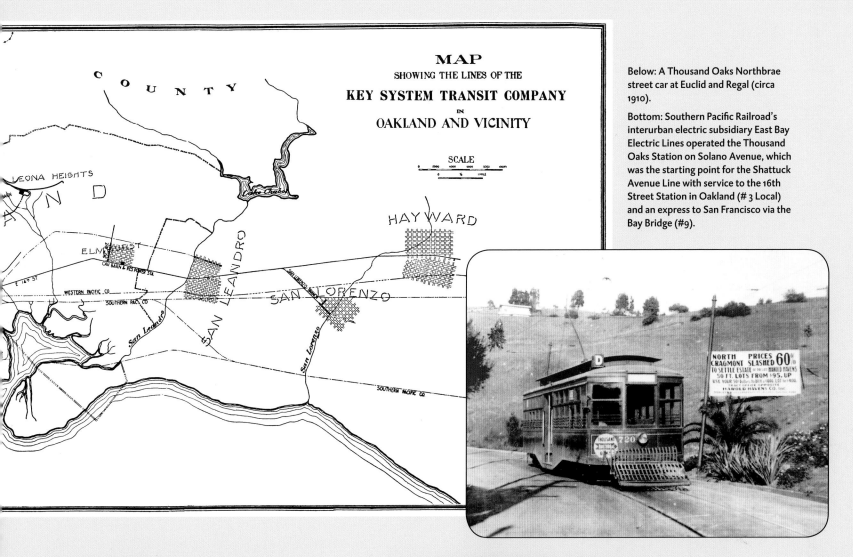

MAP
SHOWING THE LINES OF THE
KEY SYSTEM TRANSIT COMPANY
IN
OAKLAND AND VICINITY

SCALE

Below: A Thousand Oaks Northbrae street car at Euclid and Regal (circa 1910).

Bottom: Southern Pacific Railroad's interurban electric subsidiary East Bay Electric Lines operated the Thousand Oaks Station on Solano Avenue, which was the starting point for the Shattuck Avenue Line with service to the 16th Street Station in Oakland (# 3 Local) and an express to San Francisco via the Bay Bridge (#9).

neighborhoods who worked in Oakland and San Francisco. At its peak in the 1940s, the Key System had sixty-six miles of tracks. In the late 1950s a significant portion of the Key System was bought up by National City Lines (a consortium that included General Motors, Standard Oil, and Firestone) and dismantled to encourage people to buy cars and to increase bus sales. The Key System was sold to Alameda County Transit in 1960 and nowadays many bus routes continue to use the original route names.

IV. MELDING ARCHITECTURE WITH THE ROCKS

IF THE HILLSIDE CLUB HAD HAD ITS WAY, the Berkeley Hills might have been filled with rustic houses. Instead there are French Norman cottages, brick Storybook-style homes, more Colonials than you'd expect, and modern redwood abstractions. Yet all of these styles have managed to embrace the rocks.

BUILDING WITH ROCK

The Bay Area never took to stone as a major building material. Redwood was too plentiful. But local stone was incorporated into foundations and used for chimneys and facades. Its use is even more noticeable in retaining walls, ceremonial pillars and gates, and stone fireplaces in parks and private yards throughout the Berkeley Hills.

Over the years, stone has been quarried throughout the hills, including at what is now La Loma Park (near Quarry Road, naturally), at Cerritos Canyon at the end of today's Vincente Avenue, in the vicinity of today's Grizzly Peak Boulevard, and at two locations in El Cerrito, one at the present-day recycling center, the other at today's Camp Herms Boy Scout Camp. Much of the rock that went into

Menlo Place, one of the backstreets of Thousand Oaks, holds a gem of a boulder that supports a massive pine.

Berkeley Hills pillars is graywacke, chosen because it's easy to work. But rhyolite, serpentinite, chert, and other rocks can also be spotted.

John Galen Howard, the architect who oversaw the design of the University of California, designed superb pillars, entry gates, and streetcar waiting areas for Duncan McDuffie's Claremont neighborhood. They set the standard for similar work by McDuffie and other developers throughout the hills and remain neighborhood landmarks a century later.

In south Berkeley, wonderful stone retaining walls and walks can be found on Hillside Avenue, constructed by an Italian stonemason around 1907 for William Henry Smyth's Fernwald estate. In north Berkeley, Hawthorne Terrace above Cedar Street boasts a block-long stone wall of notable charm.

Berkeley's parks remain prime spots for fans of stonework. Live Oak Park, the city's first "natural" park, established in 1914, contains stone fireplaces and benches. John Hinkel Park, donated to the city by businessman John Hinkel in 1919, features an im-

mense stone fireplace that was once the site for community celebrations but is today largely ignored.

In Richmond, Alvarado Park (today the Alvarado Staging Area of Wildcat Canyon Regional Park), has wonderful stone bridges, picnic areas, and pavilions built of local stone by the Works Progress Administration during the Depression.

In the early days of development of these upscale neighborhoods, rhyolite and, especially, graywacke rock scattered throughout the Berkeley Hills was used in all manner of construction projects, from picnic shelters and entrance pillars to fireplaces and retaining walls.

FIRST BAY TRADITION

The First Bay Tradition (1880s to 1930s) refers not to a style, but to an attitude—close to nature, though not always; often idiosyncratic, sometimes jocular; rustic and vernacular, yet sophisticated; sometimes brown-shingled or wooden board-and-batten, more often stucco; occasionally incorporating Gothic trefoils and classical columns. The First Bay Tradition could be very approximately described as comprising Bay Area interpretations of the Arts and Crafts style.

A Historic Chalet Lives among the Rocks

L. John Harris's house isn't the easiest place to live. Northbrae rhyolite boulders buried deep in the earth surround it on four sides, lurk beneath its foundation, and impose their will on inhabitants and visitors. The house is downslope from the road, and the only ways in are a pair of rocky trails that swerve past mossy multicolored rocks, some topped with trees, many with wildflowers. The magic of the house, its setting, and its history make up for the inconvenience. "The rustic rock path sets a tone for what I think the house was meant to be," Harris says.

Harris lives in one of the earliest and historically most important houses in Thousand Oaks. Built in 1910, it was the home of Mark Daniels, the landscape architect, sometimes-architect, editor, writer, and longtime booster who helped design the entire neighborhood for its developer, John H. Spring. Daniels lived there until 1914, when he moved to Yosemite National Park to serve as the park's superintendent.

"Does this appeal to you as a charming and effective site for a modern hillside home?" Daniels asked readers of *California Magazine* in 1915. The question appeared beneath a photograph of a

The First Bay Tradition refers not to a style, but to an attitude.

The house that Mark Daniels built is literally wedged between boulders on Yosemite Avenue.

"Does this appeal to you as a charming and effective site for a modern hillside home?"

Massive boulders surround the Mark Daniels house on all four sides. Just as Daniels was sensitive to the constraints and opportunities such a rocky site allows, subsequent owners—first the Wentworths and now John Harris— have integrated natural features as they remodeled. From the entranceway to the lower garden, the view of rocks and rock walls harmonizes with the structure once described as a "Swiss chalet that seems intimately appropriate with such a rugged setting."

gnarled oak whose limbs scratch at the sky above a rock-strewn hillside, a rough-hewn stone stairway, and an imposing concrete Greek urn that still stands at the foot of Berkeley's Indian Trail.

The scene certainly appealed to Daniels, who built his own home just a few blocks away. More than just another house, Daniels's barnlike, Swiss chalet–style Berkeley brown-shingle served as an example to follow, in both its architecture and its treatment of the land around it.

"There are many such locations in California," Daniels continued in *California Magazine*, "restricted subdivisions for home seekers who desire something distinctive as a dwelling place." In fact, many of the homes that were built over the next three decades in Thousand Oaks made use of the Berkeley Rocks as "something distinctive."

> Daniels's home is everything a rocky hill could want— low-key, low-slung, and deferential.

Daniels (1881–1952) also designed trendsetting neighborhoods at Forest Hill and Seacliff in San Francisco, worked on 17-Mile Drive in Pebble Beach, and helped set the standards for landscape design and architecture in the national parks by serving two years as landscape engineer for Yosemite, and later for the entire National Park Service.

Daniels's home is everything a rocky hill could want—low-key, low-slung, and deferential. "This house, when they built it, they basically didn't touch the land," says landscape designer and stonemason David Liu, who spent more than a year designing and building terrace walls below the house, using nothing—or almost nothing—except rocks from the site.

Liu has created many a stone wall and has done much work throughout the Berkeley Hills. But

The rough stone pathway on the western side of the Mark Daniels house leads up to a small soot-lined cave where Ohlone artifacts are reported to have been found. Daniels selected this spot and in 1910 built one of the first and finest houses in the Thousand Oaks neighborhood; his house embodies the "build with nature" philosophy of the Hillside Club.

"You get used to the inconvenience."

he's never seen anything quite as rockin' as the Daniels house. "This is the most unusual house in all Berkeley," he says. "Most houses that have big rocks have two big rocks. Look at this! Nothing's been touched!"

That is, of course, the way Daniels wanted it. "The art of the landscape architect consists more in knowing what not to do than what to do," he wrote in *California Magazine*. "In other words, he must seek to retain the natural effects of the setting and, where changes are essential to utility, to disguise man's handiwork as much as possible. It is merely obedience to the familiar rule—'true art is to conceal art.'"

It's inconvenient to live hemmed in by rocks, but that's what makes it special. "You're living among nature," Liu says. "You're not living on a property that's been cut into the hillside. John would rather go to the trouble of stepping on uneven stones to get to his house, rather than a regular sidewalk. You get used to the inconvenience. But does John resent it? No! He loves it!"

"The rustic rock path," Harris says, "sets a tone for what I think the house was meant to be."

Designed in 1916 by architect Noble Newsom (of Newsom & Newsom) on land that was a gift from his father-in-law, John Spring, this house abuts what was listed on an early map as Tunnel Rock. This massive pile of Northbrae rhyolite is one of the hidden rock gems of Thousand Oaks. Originally the lot was not considered valuable, despite the beautiful boulder, as it did not have a view of the Bay.

BUILT ON A ROCK

Faced with a boulder-laden lot, some Berkeley builders chose to embrace the unavoidable and make the rocks a prominent part of both building and landscape design. (Perhaps the most striking example of this practice is the Mark Daniels house featured earlier in this chapter.) Floors were cantilevered over the chunks of rock breaking through the ground beside a foundation's footings (as in the house pictured below). Stucco walls molded themselves to the silhouettes of massive boulders. In other cases rocks that were too big to remove were downplayed entirely—hidden beneath a house's skirts in basements and even garages.

Above: The owner of this Shattuck Avenue house removed a basement wall during a renovation to reveal most of this massive rock under the house's front. He also exposed the other end of this boulder, making it a feature wall inside the basement (as shown on page 75).

Many Berkeley rocks straddle property boundaries, bonding neighbors who share a reverence for their rock's beauty. In this instance, the owners were each happy to keep their boulder free of fences and walls.

There is no hiding the boulder that dominates the basement garage in the Tickner house on Vincente Avenue. This house features several such massive exposed rocks.

The rock fills half the garage like a gray behemoth.

As houses are remodeled and basements are excavated in the quest for more space, homeowners are finding unexpected rocks and boulders. Once unveiled, the rocks can become the crowning feature of a room. The renovator of this Menlo Place house decided to feature opposite ends of the same rock in a shower and, through the wall, in the billiard room.

This house on Shattuck Avenue sits atop a massive North-brae rhyolite boulder, and for years its connection to the rock was only subtly obvious. When the current owner renovated, he exposed the rock under the floor of the living room to the outside by removing the enclosing wall. Where the rock emerges into the house, the use of spot lighting makes the stairs down to the basement resemble the entrance to a grotto.

A Julia Morgan Home on Thousand Oaks Boulevard

Julia Morgan, who designed San Simeon for William Randolph Hearst, knew what to do with a dramatic site. As anyone who visits Hearst Castle knows, her answer wasn't to blend in. A building in Morgan's mature style is relaxed, self-assured, even bold—but respectful of nature.

On a rock-and-oak-filled lot on Thousand Oaks Boulevard, she created a Mediterranean-style home whose front doorway is dramatically framed by natural rocks. The home's arched doorways and windows don't copy the shape of the boulders but harmonize with them subtly and well.

"Being in this house is like being inside something alive …"

The site has rocks in front and to the side. In the rear is a giant boulder that the owner, who has lived there for years, calls Big Poppa. To her, the rocks, the house, the stone walls, and the oaks that clamber over the rocks and form a canopy together create a mystical place, one she strives to protect. "Being in this house is like being inside something alive," she says. "This house lives; it breathes."

Designed by Julia Morgan, the Ralph Eltse house was built in 1915. Morgan located it at the far back of the lot to take advantage of the beautiful live oaks and large boulders. At the insistence of the client, this Mediterranean Revival house has an unusual floor plan: not a single room has four ninety-degree angles.

This large boulder set well back from the street is shared by two houses. Flat space is hard to come by in the Berkeley Hills, so the ample lawn makes this lot a prize even without the boulder. The rock wall oozes water from a natural spring (opposite), helping keep the surrounding garden lush.

Years of landscaping heighten the effect of the wood shingles and exposed timber beams of houses designed to blend in with these surroundings.

Boulder Forms a Backyard Amphitheater in a First Bay Tradition House

The mountain of blueschist that forms a backdrop for a natural amphitheater in Bill and Erica Roberts's backyard must be one of the largest rocks that remains hidden from the street in Berkeley. Their son got married at its foot, Christmas Revels dancers have rehearsed there, and family and friends have used the site to mark the passing of loved ones. "It's a very special place," Bill says.

The rock is imposing, but it shares the hillside with a mix of material that covers up a spring—

and history soon proved that the site was far from stable. The family that built the house in the 1920s also built another house atop the rock, one corner over the rock, one over the spring. By the 1950s, the house was the studio and home of David Park, whose boldly painted portraits of jazz musicians and bathers in the 1950s defined the Bay Area Figurative style. One day the house started to slide, its foundations most likely undermined by the spring. Park got out in time when the bay windows bowed out and the timbers cracked.

Today, remains of the second house can be found in shards beneath the Roberts's backyard and hidden beneath jungle on the uninhabited rock.

"The Rocks" Lords It Over Tunnel Road

John Hudson Thomas's "Wintermute House," built in 1913 atop the most prominent rock in Berkeley's Claremont neighborhood, was immediately dubbed "The Rocks," an inscription that can still be seen at its entry. It was one of the first houses in the neighborhood.

When the house was built, the promontory overlooked a quiet valley. Today that valley is Tunnel Road, the main route between Berkeley and Walnut Creek, and cars whiz by too quickly for drivers to spot the rock. That doesn't bother owner David Teece, whose home sits far back from the road.

The original landscaping took advantage of the local rocks in a series of rock-bordered paths winding down the hill, rock benches, and even a faux rock grotto, now used to store firewood. When Teece does rock work, he sticks to local rock whenever possible. Rock from the Sierras, he says, is "colder and harder," the local rock "softer and more organic."

"Why would I bring the Sierra rocks in here when I can have the local rocks? I like their warmth."

The dramatic rocks of Wintermute House (also known as "The Rocks") are best seen from the east side of Tunnel Road in the Claremont neighborhood. These formations are made of Leona rhyolite, which is much older and more friable than the Northbrae rhyolite that makes up the majority of the boulders in north Berkeley.

HIDDEN LANDMARKS

We know from old photos that in the early 1900s the hillsides in and around Berkeley were mostly bare, but today they are heavily vegetated and urbanized. Some of the area's most imposing and celebrated boulders now lie on private land, hidden behind high front fences and thickets of vegetation or tucked away in backyards. Monument Rock, once a prominent feature of the landscape, is now shrouded by trees and houses and is topped by a deck. Rockridge Rock in North Oakland, which was a picnickers' destination, bridges two lots and presents a much more modest public face than it once did.

Even some publicly accessible boulders, like Murieta Rock on the corner of Cutting and Arlington in El Cerrito, are rendered nearly invisible by dint of development. Had the proposed park in Thousand Oaks been approved in 1908, many more massive Berkeley rocks would have been available for the public to gaze upon and enjoy—and this neighborhood would have been very different indeed.

Carved out of the hill at the top of Solano Avenue, the Northbrook Tunnel once had the tracks of the Southern Pacific Railroad running through it. Today from the path alongside the road one can see how the boulder was cut to make the tunnel. Over the fence, a sister rock shares the backyard of houses on Mendocino Avenue.

Another hidden outcropping on Vincente Avenue in Thousand Oaks, this massive Northbrae rhyolite boulder dominates the back and side yards of this house. Ohlone artifacts, including a portable stone mortar and pestle, were discovered here during a basement renovation.

Historic rocks in Berkeley have often been integrated into houses—perhaps none more so than Monument Rock on Vincente Avenue. This massive rock once marked the northeast corner of the Peralta land grant.

PERIOD REVIVAL HOUSES OF
THE EARLY TWENTIETH CENTURY

Many historians regard the Period Revival and Storybook houses that fill so much of the Berkeley Hills as late variants of the Bay Area Arts and Crafts Movement. It's a tempting proposition. Maybeck, after all, designed wonderful Gothic halls, Julia Morgan created the incomparable San Simeon for William Randolph Hearst, and John Hudson Thomas dropped his early, modern style for English cottages.

But can Period Revival be regarded as a local style at all? The craze for English cottages and Norman half-timbers swept the country in the 1920s, and examples every bit as quirky as those in the Berkeley Hills can be found in Buffalo and Birmingham.

A Manor House Built on a Rock

W. W. Dixon, one of the Bay Area's most prolific designers, designed a European fantasy—a bit of Spain here, some France and England there—for a rocky site in the Berkeley Hills in 1929. Now the home of Henriette Zabin, it has the appearance of a manor house growing out of the rocks.

There are immense rocks in front, large ones behind, stone bridges, curved rock terraces, and walls of local stone. A perennial creek winding downhill through a rock-strewn bed adds a naturalistic touch. Like many of Berkeley's 1920s homes, this one came with an outdoor stone fireplace ideal for barbecuing spits of meat. Though few remain in use, Henriette Zabin still uses hers.

Keeping her rocks free of brush and open to the air takes time, but Zabin says it's worth it. "Oh, God, I love rocks. I don't know why," she says. "I like the feel of them."

This Period Revival house is perched atop a massive rhyolite boulder and situated among other boulders along the stream that flows through the property.

One Thing for Adults, Quite Another for Kids

The Stevensons have lived with their rock for more than fifty years, but Lois is still learning about it, including things she'd rather not know—for example, that her children rarely got to the front door using the stairs. "I wouldn't ever use the stairs to come up," her son Conrad says. "It was a straight climb from the bottom."

The Stevenson home, a grand visitor from Normandy, has stone stairs cut through the rock with an angular banister provided by Conrad's brother.

Despite the danger, Lois has always loved the rocks. "It's just the nearness of them," she says.

Though not the largest, this boulder bulging out into the footpath and split by a well-used stairway is one of the most noticeable on Berkeley's rockiest street (Vincente Avenue).

The Guardian Rocks (as they are listed on an early map) are massive but seem in balance with the historic Villa Filice, one of Berkeley's grandest mansions, which occupies a one-third-acre lot on The Alameda. The real estate literature for a recent sale of this property names the three-story boulder Sentry Rock. Regardless of what the rock is called, it is one of the most prominent and beautifully lansdcaped rocks on private land in Berkeley.

SECOND BAY TRADITION

The Second Bay Tradition (mid-1930s to 1960s) was both a celebration and a refutation of the Euro-

pean-based International style. Second Bay Tradition houses are spare, in keeping with the Interna-

tional style, with walls of glass, open plans, and attention to function. But they are far from cool and decidedly not international.

Second Bay Tradition houses glory in redwood and love natural stone.

Borrowing from Frank Lloyd Wright and such First Bay Tradition pioneers as Maybeck,

modernist Second Bay Tradition homes owe much to local vernacular styles, which is anathema to

International style purists. They borrow from barns and adobes, use gabled roofs as well as flat roofs,

and artfully blend into the landscape. They glory in redwood and love natural stone.

A Roger Lee House in Thousand Oaks

If Bay Tradition architecture is about harmonizing with nature, then the house on a rocky Vin-

cente Avenue site designed in 1950 by architect Roger Lee looks at first like anything but Bay Tradition architecture. And it's true that Lee's designs—rectangular, glassy, severe—often seem more International style cool than Berkeley redwood warm.

The original house, typical of Lee at his most cost conscious, is a long, single-story wood and glass box sitting on a pad as flat as any urban lot in Paris or Manhattan. But the setting is magical. From the street

you can't see the house at all, just a jaunty carport, a forest of oaks, and boulders of Northbrae

rhyolite climbing a treacherous slope.

Typical of Lee is the house's wall of glass. Instead of staring out at bridges and the Bay, however,

these windows face rock. The view is dramatic enough for the current owners, Mary Ford and Rob

Lewis, who will never forget their first night there.

Dinner was ready, rain was pouring down, and Rob discovered what happens when Northbrae rhyolite meets water. "The rocks changed completely in color," he says. "This red came out that was like, Wow!" Rob and Mary set their dinner down on the living room floor and ate while admiring the rocks.

"The rocks make me feel like I'm on a real piece of land, not on a little postage-stamp lawn," Mary says. "I feel like I'm on a big hill. It's just so not man-made. Nature wins. Nature predominates."

A Ranch Style House Learns to Live with a Rock

When a local builder decided to construct a pair of modern homes atop a rock on Vincente

Avenue in 1951, "the neighbors thought he was out of his mind," Robin Tickner says. And it wasn't

only because the site seemed impossible.

"This was a very avant-garde house," she says of one of the two, which she has come to own,

"very much different from anything in the neighborhood."

Today, the house seems a model of coexistence, it's mid-1950s modernism blending easily with

the local rock, which provides tasteful accents in the backyard and a natural deck out front. "My husband and I still sit out there and have our gin and tonics," Robin says.

The rock also fills half the garage like a gray behemoth. Originally the builder tried to blow up the rock, but when windows shattered up and down the street, lawyers were consulted and the blasting stopped.

Robin grew up across the street and roller-skated in the house's garage as a girl. When the home came up for sale, she and her husband, Walt, jumped. They love the house's combination of openness and solidity. Its structural steel is bolted to the rock. "If this house goes," Robin boasts, "all of Berkeley is gone."

And they love their rock. "The rock has its own even temperature," Robin says, caressing the outcrop in the garage. "Feel it: It's warm. That's not a cold rock. Even in the wintertime the rock holds its heat and helps warm the house."

The Man Who Talks to Trees

In the mid-1960s, architect John Fornoff and family spent months looking for a special site for their home. "I've got to have something with a rock or a tree on it," Fornoff vowed.

The Fornoffs scored big when John spotted a grove of bay trees in El Cerrito and approached their ivy-covered base. "You ought to see what's under here," he called to his wife. "You can't believe it."

What he discovered was an immense mountain of schist topped by dozens of trees that form an unbroken canopy. "I never met a rock I didn't like," Fornoff says.

Early on a neighbor strolled by and said, "Boy, you sure have got yourself a big job, getting rid of that rock."

"Boy, you sure have got yourself a big job, getting rid of that rock."

Fornoff designed an open-plan, open-beamed, low-cost wooden structure that he describes as "an upside-down boat." "My wife and I built the house ourselves," he says, "literally."

The house overlooks Wildcat Canyon to the east, but the view to the west is just as enchanting—a close-up of the rock. He's made friends with the birds and gopher snakes that inhabit the forested rock, and he enjoys the sense of security the rock provides. The laurels hover precipitously over his roof but have never fallen. He asks them not to. "I call myself the man who talks to trees."

This Japanese-influenced house tucked away in El Cerrito is one of the most modern to embrace such a rocky site. Perched on steel pillars on the northern side, it has a magnificent view of the San Francisco Bay. Seen from the road, the house melds into the Leona rhyolite boulders; when viewed from the back (opposite), it seems to fly above the rocks.

THIRD BAY TRADITION

The Third Bay Tradition, rooted in the work of Charles Moore and Joseph Esherick, produced houses that were as woodsy as the First and Second, but more abstract and perhaps even more informal, with dramatic vertical spaces. The forms of a Third Bay Tradition house tend to be boxy, roofs angular and shedlike, windows large, oddly placed, and flush against the walls.

In the mid-1970s, architect Logan Hopper put a Third Bay Tradition house on a prominent site next to Indian Rock Park. The house is stark and angular, yet as comfortable and woodsy as a vacation chalet, similar to those found at Sea Ranch, where this style of architecture seems most at home. But it also seems at home among the rocks.

It sits on rocks, looks out on rocks, and uses a rock as an extension of its deck. Dan Rossi and Robin Miller's children, Benji and Talia, often climb onto the rock to enjoy the view onto Indian Rock Park.

V. LANDSCAPING WITH THE BERKELEY ROCKS

THE ROCKS OF BERKELEY ARE INCREASINGLY WELL TENDED. From homeowner after homeowner you hear the same story: "When we bought this house, we didn't know the rocks were here, they were so covered with ivy (or brush or weeds or muck)."

Clearly, people in the Berkeley Hills appreciate what rocks can add to a garden. "Rocks are always good in a garden," says Ann Luse, who lives in the old Charles Keeler home in the Claremont district. "They give it solidity and structure. It's not until you have that, that you can install little decorative things, like flowers."

Landscaping with rocks means different things for different gardeners. Many prefer the natural look, a hillside of rock overshadowed by oaks. Others liven up their rocks with color—camellias, roses, wisteria growing from the rock or next to it.

One owner planted an American Victorian cast-iron stag on her rock, a prominent spot in the neighborhood. "It's been a nice icebreaker," she says, helping her meet many new neighbors.

Often people use local rock to create walls, but sometimes they bring in rock from outside— which runs the risk of looking like something from outside. Neil Collier, a landscape designer and

The spine of this very fractured outcrop has been landscaped into a beautiful
rock garden that flows over the ridge on the northern border of Kensington.

103

stonemason who runs Live Oak Landscaping, often brings in Napa rhyolite to repair existing walls of Northbrae rhyolite, but the slight color difference does present a problem. "It's nice to keep to the same kind of rock," he cautions.

Stonemasonry is an art, he says. "It's a difficult thing to teach. Either somebody has it or they don't have it. It's a bit like doing jigsaw puzzles."

WORKING WITH ROCK

Removing a rock—or a portion of a rock—is no easy task, as John Harris's crew found out when they carved out chunks from a Northbrae rhyolite boulder in his Thousand Oaks yard to make way for a deck. The work was backbreaking.

Liu compares building a wall to weaving fabric.

Stonemason David Liu.

Rock wall at the Mark Daniels house.

None of the rock that was jackhammered away will go to waste. Much of it has already gone into the retaining walls for a series of terraces that landscape designer and stonemason David Liu began constructing below the Mark Daniels house, today owned by John Harris. "Some of them are heavy," says Liu. "But they're not impossible to move." Individual rocks often weigh fifty to two hundred pounds, so Liu rolls them whenever he can and tries to avoid lifting. Each wall also contains hundreds of tiny stones, put in for looks.

Liu is a master of dry wall construction—fitting stones together like a jigsaw puzzle, without mortar, or using mortar only for special purposes. It's a time-consuming, exacting process, as much an art as a science. The stones have to fit together in a way that is both structurally sound and aesthetically appealing. Aesthetic integrity is why Liu prefers building such walls on his own.

"This is a one-man sort of thing. If I had someone else do it, it would look different. It's a signature," he says. "Each mason does things slightly differently. Sometimes you see existing walls, then someone adds onto it, you can see exactly where the new wall starts even though they used the same ingredients. The handprint is different."

Liu, who fell in love with rocks years ago when he was working in the Sierras, compares building a wall to weaving fabric. How the stones fit together provides strength. The mason's job is to avoid running seams—gaps between rocks that run vertically through the wall.

Above: In the 1890s, highly skilled Italian stone-masons faced the bridge over Prospect Creek and the walls along the street with local rhyolite rock.

Opposite: David Liu and some of his handiwork: a new stone facade on Thousand Oaks Boulevard.

Construction goes smoothly when Liu has a good stack of rocks to work with, as he did when the boulder was first broken up. Then it's simply a matter of standing back and sizing up the available stones for size and fit, texture and color. "I have in mind the exact size," Liu says. "I go to my rock pile and look for it. I work with the shape of the rock until I start running out of rock." After that, he says, "You just do the best you can, use smaller and smaller rocks, do a little chipping."

Liu loves Berkeley's Northbrae rhyolite for its subtlety. "It has a very nice texture," he says, rubbing his hand across the rock that looms above Harris's front door. "It's porous. You can see this very light part here, polished by erosion. It's not a monotone. It has different colors—reddish, rust, salmon—because of the iron oxide. This part here is almost like marble. There's green, because of the lichen. That white part isn't porous; nothing can grow there. But in this part, where the water penetrates, lichen and moss grow.

"If it were just pure granite, in this small setting, it wouldn't work so well. In Yosemite the granite adds to the grandeur of things. But here, with more texture, it's easier on the eye."

Liu also warns against bringing in exotic rocks. "You try to work within the environment that already exists," Liu says. "You don't want to modify it too much. You don't want to go outside and introduce an element that's not compatible with the site."

As he drives through the neighborhood, Liu spots occasional examples of foreign rocks that disrupt the landscape. But for the most part, people get it. "People around here," he says, "love their rocks."

ALL THINGS INDIGENOUS

Lee and Lone Coleman's 1920s half-timbered masterpiece in Thousand Oaks looks like something

from Great Britain. But their rock work is nothing but Berkeley.

Their rock garden is built around natural outcroppings, and the stone walls and benches are

constructed of stone dug up from beneath the house during construction, or scrounged from neigh-

bors. Lee finds discarded stones in dumpsters and abandoned

along curbs. "If I find them and they're the real thing, if they're

rock from here, I grab them and collect them," he says. "I figure

sooner or later I'll have something to do with them.

"I see it as a part of making the house special. You use the

material here to express who you are and what you believe in.

It's not just a landscaping material. It's much more than that."

Their garden is a delight, but the Colemans never brag. "It's

not like we had a grand plan and carried it out," Lone says.

"Our idea," Lee says, "was to show off the rock."

"You use the material here to express who you are and what you believe in."

A CORNER OF NEW ENGLAND IN THE EL CERRITO HILLS

Some rocks win fame on their own, and some get some help from their owners. Don Tieck, a fan of all things clapboard and white, and Alex Adelman, who prefers the shades of the Southwest, turned the rock their homes share on Arlington Boulevard into paired landmarks—a New England lighthouse next to a field of cacti, each sitting on a notable rock.

Life in California can be what you want it to be, Sonoran Desert here, Cape Cod there. Today, Tieck notes, "It's a neighborhood phenomenon."

In itself, the rock is imposing—Arlington wisely swerves to avoid it. But over the years it lost some luster. When Don Tieck bought his mid-1940s house, the rock was invisible, hidden by ivy, juniper, and worse. The house, too, was lackluster and nondescript.

Once he revealed the rock, he says, "It started screaming 'cactus!' at me."

But Tieck, who has traveled widely in New England, transformed it into a Cape Cod or Nantucket sea captain's Colonial, complete with shutters, eagles over the door and on the gazebo, a deck, and a lighthouse with a working strobe. "I thought, hey, I'd like to have a lighthouse sticking out of a rock by my deck."

Tieck's next door neighbor, Alex Adelman, provided the Southwest motif by bringing in 250 different varieties of cactus. His obsession started shortly after he bought the house, high on a rise above Arlington. The rock was hidden by pampas grass. "My mantra of the day was, restore the rock." Once he revealed the rock, he says, "It started screaming 'cactus!' at me, and it said, 'Southwest.'"

A BONSAI ROCK SUPERSIZED

The marriage of oak and rock in front of Stephen and Doris Chun's Shattuck Avenue home seems almost too perfect. No wild limbs here, just a perfect rounded crown on the live oak perched in the middle of their rock.

The harmony of the scene is a marriage of nature and art. "The acorn popped in there and found a spot," Stephen says. Then art took over. The Chuns, who love Asian art and volunteer at the Asian Art Museum, keep the tree carefully pruned to produce its classic canopy and allow for light and air. "It's like a bonsai," Stephen says. "It has that very Asian flavor to it."

The Chuns point out that the rock and tree provide two of three essential components found in classical Chinese paintings. The third is provided when it rains (or when uphill neighbors water) and the runoff streams down the front of their rock.

When the Chuns bought the house, "The big rock was completely covered with the vine, so all we saw was the tree," Stephen says. "No rock. Nothing. It was like a jungle grew over the rock." They cleared the brush and the rock appeared. "That was quite a pleasant surprise," he says, "and a joy to see that."

The rock and tree provide two of three essential components found in classical Chinese paintings.

ZACH PINE

Zach Pine, an environmental sculptor some of whose works evoke those of Andy Goldsworthy, used a cracked boulder on Colusa Avenue in north Berkeley in this piece from 2003. Knitted together by lengths of eucalyptus bark, the rock for a time ceased being a monument to permanence and another facet emerged: Berkeley's rocks are the fixed points around which houses, gardens, parks, and neighborhoods rise and fall, but they are transitory too. Many of the rocks came here from someplace else, and they'll keep emerging and crumbling away over the eons.

While some Bay Area home owners have to ship in rocks to add interest to their yards, many homes in Thousand Oaks have plenty on-site. The secret is working with the trees and vegetation to make a complementary setting.

ROCKS GIVE FOCUS TO A THOUSAND OAKS GARDEN

Harry Delmer's garden is very much the product of Harry Delmer's muscles. "Let's just say I was the tectonic force that moved the rocks around," he says. But the net result is something closer to nature than it was when he found it more than two decades ago.

His neighborhood in Thousand Oaks is rock central, with more rocks per house than anywhere else in town. Old-timers recall the days when blasts indicated neighbors doing their best to level a rock.

In Delmer's backyard, these blasted shards were used to create heavily mortared rock terraces and a wall. They were too mortared for Delmer, who wanted more rock and less cement. He's replaced the mortared retaining walls with dry wall construction, rearranged his loose rocks, and planted succulents on his backyard boulder.

Rocks and a hillside make gardening easy, he says. "A typical suburban lot—it's hard making interesting landscape. When you have an upward slope and tons of rock, you can't miss. It provides infinite possibilities for beautiful landscaping."

"When you have an upward slope and tons of rock, you can't miss."

A ROCK WITH TWO FACES

Like many of the rocks of Berkeley, the Hussains' rock on Marin Avenue is well-known. "Oh! The house with the rock!" people exclaim. "It's a very popular rock," I. K. Hussain says.

"For ten years before I bought this house, I knew the rock," he says. "It's very unique. It gives the house something distinctive. It's like a fence. It gives some privacy, but at the same time it's not too high."

"It's a very popular rock."

But unless they visit Hussain and his wife, Fatima, passersby see only the rugged rock that drops to the sidewalk like a mountain wall. The civilized rock, with its purple-flowered princess plant, its well-tended olive tree, its orange flowers, is seen only from the front yard of their 1920s English cottage. Their two daughters used to play on the rock, and friends would sunbathe on its flat surface, warmed by hours of sunlight. "The space is usable," Hussain says. "Most rocks are not."

Above: This natural rhyolite plinth works beautifully in the Japanese-style garden adjacent to Great Stoneface Park.

Right: A chunk of ancient Leona rhyolite dominates this garden near Tunnel Road.

Opposite: A sculpture on The Alameda evokes a common garden nuisance in the Berkeley Hills—the herds of hungry deer.

This rustic front garden's stone path and stairway weave through large moss-covered boulders to the Tudor-style house on top of the knoll. An upright boulder is carved with the house's name (left).

Boulders and oaks dominate the vast yard of this Spanish-style house on Yosemite Avenue. Dennis Makishima, a bonsai master gardener, tends some of the smaller trees on this lot, nurturing the relationship between the rocks and the garden.

VI. LANDMARK ROCKS

MANY ROCKS HAVE PLAYED AN IMPORTANT ROLE IN LOCAL HISTORY or served as neighborhood landmarks. Although only a few have been declared official landmarks, with the protection such designation provides, Berkeley's affection for its rocks is evident in the special names bestowed on individual rocks. And the city's many rock parks make it easy for the public to enjoy its rocks.

THE SAVIORS OF PICNIC ROCK

Grand and historical as they are, almost all the rocks in the Berkeley Hills are privately owned. Moreover, there are no laws to protect privately owned rocks, as there are for creeks and certain trees. Owners can chip them, mine them, even demolish them. Or they can try. No environmental impact report is needed.

There is, however, an exception. Sutliff Rock in Thousand Oaks was declared a Berkeley site of merit by the Landmarks Preservation Commission in 1990 because of "its special value to the

Easy access to its high, wide apex made Sutliff Rock, or Picnic Rock, a popular gathering spot (on Santa Rosa Avenue) for families and children in Berkeley's early days. There was even a telescope mounted on its summit.

neighborhood and the city as a site of historical, cultural, and educational value." It is the only rock in Berkeley so designated.

During a battle that lasted for decades a series of owners tried unsuccessfully to build a house alongside this rock that locals say is a neighborhood landmark and de facto park. Maps going back to 1915 identify the outcropping as Picnic Rock.

Although the battle was successful in protecting Picnic Rock from development, for many years there were no real winners. From the late 1970s until very recently, the rock was off-limits to all, and cordoned off behind a chain-link fence. And hanging over the neighbor's head was the threat that the rock might one day be developed.

In 2005, however, a pair of saviors bought the rock. "We bought it for the sole purpose of preserving it and to protect the interesting flora on it," says Eric Wilson, who lives across from the rock with his wife, Katie. Today, the Wilsons allow neighbors to visit, as well as people who are studying plants, rocks, or anthropology. But Picnic Rock isn't open to the public without permission.

This story suggests how strongly Berkeley's residents feel about their neighborhood rocks, and it also shows what can happen when private property rights conflict with community sentiment and history. "It was heartbreaking when it was locked up," says Robin Tickner, who grew up in the neighborhood. "I spent many hours just hanging on the rock. It's where I thought through many of my growing-up problems."

FOUNDERS' ROCK

Concert-goers hustling to catch a band at the Greek Theater often hurry past a nearby outcrop of rock that's hidden by shrubbery and oaks and easy to ignore. But no one could miss seeing the rock in the mid-nineteenth century, when it overlooked a mostly undeveloped plain that stretched to San Francisco Bay.

It was natural, therefore, for the founders of the College of California (today the University of California) to gather at this prominent site when it was time to give birth to the school. On April 16,

1860, College of California trustees dedicated the campus site while standing in front of the rock. Six years later, again in front of the rock, the trustees chose the name "Berkeley" for the new town, after Bishop George Berkeley of England, author of the poem that declared, "Westward the course of empire takes its way."

The rock remained an important gathering spot for years. It was named to the National Register of Historic Places in 1981.

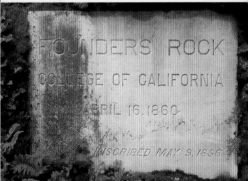

The rock was a haven for every kid in the neighborhood when it was owned by the Sutliff family, she recalls. "It was paradise. The view was spectacular. You could play all kinds of games, cowboys and Indians. You could imagine that you were on Mars. We'd have picnics up there; we would go up there as teenagers and make out. It was part of our lives."

The situation changed in the 1970s, when the family that lived next door to the rock proposed building a traditional Berkeley brown-shingle. Neighbors, citing "esthetic, historical and archeological considerations," reached deep into history to show that the rock had always been used by the public. It had been "an ideal recreational resource for generations of children and adults."

"The view was spectacular … You could imagine that you were on Mars."

Historian Edward Staniford discovered that in the 1920s the owner had a sandbox on site for local kids to use. Children had birthday parties on the rock through the twenties and thirties, he said, and neighbors watched fireworks from its peak. The owners even placed a telescope atop the rock and invited neighbors to gaze into the night sky.

University of California geologist Walter Alvarez, who later gained fame for his theory that the collision of an asteroid or comet with the earth killed off the dinosaurs, argued that natural features like rocks deserve protection just as much as cultural features, like buildings or battlefields.

The view from Picnic Rock at night.

ROCKRIDGE

In the late 1870s, long before the Oakland Hills filled with homes, picnickers flocked to a mountain of stone that developers John C. Hays and Horatio and Charles Livermore dubbed Rock Ridge. They encouraged the public to treat the site as a picnic ground, which was then a standard practice for luring would-be home buyers. The name Rockridge stuck to a neighborhood downhill from the actual rock.

A photograph in the Oakland History Room of the Oakland Library shows dozens of picnickers in their Sunday best gathered about the rock, some surveying the scene from its summit.

Back then the rock was impossible to miss, but today it's hard to find. Hidden by trees and shrubbery, and mostly behind a fence, it is shared by two homes at the corner of Glenbrook and Bowling Drives. It's still a magnificent rock, but it's best appreciated by those who own it.

Back then the rock was impossible to miss, but today it's hard to find.

Rockridge Rock now . . .

. . . and circa 1910.

MURIETA ROCK

Another once-famous rock that has lost its prominence is Murieta Rock, located on a busy corner where Arlington and Cutting Boulevards meet. The rock is named for the legendary bandit Joaquin Murieta (circa 1832–1853, if indeed he lived at all), the Robin Hood of pastoral California. It's been said that he used the rock as a lookout when his gang hid out in nearby Wildcat Canyon.

A century ago, Murieta Rock could be seen for miles around. Today, unless you get close you can't see it at all, thanks to oak trees, brush, and ivy. With a little work, this privately owned mountain of blueschist would be one of the choicest landmarks in the El Cerrito Hills. It currently serves as an informal hangout, attracting people who enjoy taking in views while drinking beer.

The fractured surfaces of Murieta Rock are indicative of its composition—it is blueschist, or metamorphosed basalt that formed deep inside the earth. Almost hidden from view by trees and defaced by graffiti, Murieta Rock would greatly benefit from some civic attention. This site provides sightseers with one of the best vantage points in the El Cerrito Hills.

BLAKE GARDEN

Blake Garden, one of the treasured spots in the Kensington Hills, provides 10.6 acres of formal gardens, woods, and trails surrounding a 1920s Mediterranean mansion that serves as home to the president of the University of California. The gardens, used as a teaching tool for landscape architecture students, are open to the public on weekdays.

And thanks to the nearby Hayward Fault, an immense boulder of glaucophane schist behind the home is a draw for geologists. "Few places on the surface of the earth have lawsonite," John Norcross, the garden's manager, says of the white veins that course through the rock. Lawsonite, named for the late Andrew Lawson, the professor of geology who came up with the names Leona and Northbrae rhyolite, is a metamorphic mineral produced only in certain fault zones. "It's emerged from the fault line over eons," Norcross says.

PRESERVING AND PROTECTING THE ROCKS

In the early years of development in the Berkeley Hills, the sites of a number of large rocks were donated to the city to become parks, as developers deemed these outcrops unsuitable for building lots. The developers also realized that proximity to such unique public spaces would add value to their remaining real estate. Over time new plots were also donated to become parks (the case with Remillard Park) and others were expanded with the acquisition of adjacent land (as with Cragmont Park).

Today north Berkeley's public rock parks are cared for by the City of Berkeley, but they can't be completely protected from vandalism and graffiti. And attitudes toward what is acceptable treatment and use of the parks are evolving all the time. In days gone by, steps and seats were carved into the rocks to give easy access to the top. This is most obvious at Indian Rock. More obscure rocks, like Grizzly Caves just off Grizzly Peak Road, are subject to all manner of desecration: from revelers showering the rocks with broken glass to taggers with spray paint marking their territory.

Climbers also have their own code of ethics about the rocks. Intentionally changing the rock (chipping off a piece to make a route easier or harder, for example) is a serious offense, but most climbers have no qualms

about leaving white gymnast's chalk all over the rocks. While these marks are not permanent, it takes a long time for them to weather away. Climbers used to place bolts in the rocks to protect climbs and create anchors for belays and top ropes. Older bolts (now unsafe because of rust and wear) are gradually being replaced or removed altogether in the spirit of the "clean climbing" philosophy that evolved in the 1980s.

There are a few individual rocks (Picnic, or Sutliff, Rock, Landmark 137; and Founders' Rock, Landmark 149) that are designated City of Berkeley Landmarks, under the Landmarks Ordinance adopted in 1974. Other man-made rhyolite rock structures, like the Northbrae Public Improvements (including the Marin Circle and Fountain), are also designated landmarks.

Above: Picnic (Sutliff) Rock.
Left: Grizzly Peak boulder.

Other notable rock structures, like the Hillside Avenue Bridge and Stone Walls, are recognized by Susan Cerny in her book *Berkeley Landmarks*. Still others, such as Indian Rock, are so prominent and integral to Berkeley culture they could be called the people's landmarks. Some privately owned rocks, like Sutliff Rock (Picnic Rock), are fenced off for reasons of liability and to preserve unique pockets of vegetation rather than just for privacy. It is possible to access this landmark rock by contacting the owners.

Left: Skull Rock.
Below: Murieta Rock.

BERKELEY'S ROCK PARKS

Although most of the Berkeley Rocks are privately owned, several choice specimens have been pre-served for public use. Many were donated by developers. Each park has something unique about it: for the climber, some of the toughest "problems" in the Bay Area at Indian Rock Park; for the historian, Indian mortar holes at Mortar Rock Park; for picnickers, a covered dining area built of rock at Cragmont Rock Park.

There's tiny Contra Costa Rock Park, just a rock—with a wonderful view over Solano Avenue and the Bay—and a small spot for picnicking. Great Stoneface Park is centered upon a rock that historic photos show once looked exactly like the face of a sleeping Indian; today the silhouette is obscure. Another pocket park is Grotto Rock Park, on Santa Barbara Road. The rock fills most of the park and has stone steps leading to wonderful views.

Contra Costa Rock Park (left and opposite below).

Climbing on Pinnacle Rock in Remillard Park (opposite above).

Marvelous afternoons can be spent hiking from park to park.

Grotto Rock Park (this page and opposite, above) once had a natural spring. Nowadays, its relative obscurity, easy path to the summit, and position above the surrounding houses make it a great spot to take in views of the San Francisco Bay or a sunset over Mount Tamalpais.

Alvarado Park in Richmond (opposite, below), once called Grand Canyon Park, is the site of the northernmost outcrop of Leona rhyolite. Many of the park's WPA-era walls and structures were built with this rock.

Remillard Park, built around the imposing Pinnacle Rock, has a playground, picnic area, and hiking trails; it's also a good rock climbing destination. The sprawling Hinkel Park has a few boulders but isn't really a "rock park"; however, don't miss its wonderful fireplace constructed of local stone.

The parks function best as part of a whole. Marvelous afternoons can be spent hiking from park to park along the network of pedestrian pathways, sidewalks, and steps that grace Berkeley and Kensington.

In Richmond, Alvarado Park (today the staging area for Wildcat Canyon Regional Park), has picnic tables set beneath

Park Visitors at the entrance to Grand Canyon Park - Now known as Alvarado Park

immense chunks of Leona rhyolite, plus rock walls, fireplaces, and pavilions built by Works Progress Administration workers in the 1930s. In El Cerrito, Canyon Trail Park and Huber Park provide rocky pleasures.

Many of the East Bay Regional Parks are awash in rocks, but none more so than Robert Sibley Volcanic Regional Preserve, where fans of geology can walk through the tilted heart of a volcanic cone to see frozen flows of basalt that are 9.5 million years old.

The once-prominent outline of the reclining indian head that gives Great Stoneface Park (pictured on this page) its name is now partially obscured by vegetation. The nose is the bulge on the flat top. You have to imagine the rest.

Opposite: This large, undercut boulder at Great Stoneface Park is classic Northbrae rhyolite. The telltale white gymnast's-chalk marks indicate there are some short but challenging climbing (bouldering) moves on this piece of rock. The park is also popular with geologists because many of the boulders show classic flow banding formations. But the most regular use of this park comes in the evening when dozens of locals come to exercise their dogs.

VII. CLIMBING

SET AGAINST HALF DOME OR EL CAPITAN, INDIAN ROCK doesn't look like much. But Berkeley's Indian, Cragmont, and Pinnacle rocks played as important a role as any Yosemite rock face in forging the modern sport of technical rock climbing.

It was at Berkeley's rocks that Dick Leonard, David Brower (later the longtime president of the Sierra Club), Jules Eichorn, Bestor Robinson, and other members of the Cragmont Climbing Club devised techniques that transformed rock climbing and allowed people to climb where no one could climb before.

"It opened people to climbs they didn't think were possible," says Dan Zimmerlin, a longtime member of the club. "They took a major step in the development of international climbing. They were really pioneers."

The saga began in the early 1930s, the start of the Depression. The Berkeley climbers, many of them lawyers, wanted to ascend the rock faces of Yosemite, but they also wanted to come back alive. Lacking the time to make multiple practice trips to the Sierras, they began on the local rocks,

Rock climbers have been training on these rocks since the 1920s. At forty feet high in some places, Cragmont Rock has the tallest face and has some of the longest climbs in the Berkeley Hills. Due to Cragmont Rock's height, most climbers use a technique called "top-roping"—relying on a rope fastened to the rock at the top of the climb—to protect themselves should they fall.

143

studying European techniques and importing pitons and carabiners from Munich because rock climbing equipment was unavailable in the States.

Soon they were attaching ropes to Indian and Cragmont rocks, practicing falls, and learning how to "traverse a high angle face without adequate footholds, relying upon jam technique in the crack beneath the overhang," Leonard reported. The goal was to ensure that if the leader fell, a companion could check the fall by hanging onto the rope, or belaying.

In belaying, the leader is tied into a rope that's attached to the rock face through pitons and carabiners and wrapped around the body of the belayer. At first the Berkeley climbers used standard European belaying techniques. But, Zimmerlin says, "Those guys said, 'We need a better technique,' and they set about to find one."

Months of experimentation led to development of the dynamic belay, in which there's some slack in the rope, which is wrapped around the belayer's hips instead of the shoulders. This provides more friction and less strain when the leader falls, and the lower center of gravity lends greater stability. It also led to a new philosophy. "The ethic in Europe," Zimmerlin says, "was the leader should not fall." But with more reliable belaying techniques, the leader could fall—safely. Climbers could thus take more risks and tackle more challenging routes. "This completely changed what they could practically climb," Zimmerlin says.

A young David Brower works on his climbing technique.

The Berkeley climbers practiced for years on the Berkeley Rocks before trying a Yosemite climb on Labor Day 1933.

Bestor Robinson wrote about the first ascent of Yosemite's Higher Cathedral Spire, noted for the "utter absence of cracks and the existence of massive overhangs." One traverse—a sideways climb—"ended at a steep crack, excellent in its climbing possibilities, but dizzily overhanging hundreds of feet of empty space," Robinson reported. Even lunch was an adventure. "There is a real thrill," he went on, "in munching an orange while perched on a one-foot ledge roped to the mountain for safety, and watching orange peels drop perpendicularly to the talus below without once touching the mountainside."

The goal was to ensure that if the leader fell, a companion could check the fall.

It took nine hours to reach the top. Robinson marveled at teammate Eichorn's "remarkable sense of balance and ability to stick to nothing." Robinson's summing up of the climb in the *Sierra Club Bulletin* also sums up the club's early philosophy, and suggests its accomplishments: "Looking back upon the climb, we found our greatest satisfaction in having demonstrated, at least to ourselves, that by the proper application of climbing technique extremely difficult ascents can be made in safety."

In addition to their early innovations in climbing techniques, members of the club also contributed to the development of nylon rope as a climbing tool while serving with the famous Tenth Mountain Division in Italy during World War II, Zimmerlin says.

In later years, nature photographer Galen Rowell joined the club and climbed the Berkeley Rocks. For many years the club was part of the Sierra Club, but the two parted ways when liability worries caused the Sierra Club to drop rock climbing as an activity.

The Berkeley Rocks still attract beginning and experienced climbers. Indian Rock attracts boulderers, who tackle interesting challenges on smaller rocks. Cragmont remains popular for top-roping, in which the climber is protected by a safety rope attached at the top of the route. The rocks may be small, but climbing them isn't easy. Mortar Rock has one route that a popular climbers guide calls "the Bay Area's hardest problem."

Allen Steck, who began climbing at Indian Rock in 1946 before making many first ascents as a mountaineer, explains the appeal of rock climbing: "It takes you away from your daily life. It shows you a new appreciation of nature. And there's the kinesthetic pleasure of it, using your body like a gymnast."

> *Mortar Rock has one route that a popular climbers guide calls "the Bay Area's hardest problem."*

Left: A climber tackles a tough stretch at Mortar Rock.

Opposite: Bouldering at Indian Rock is a very popular pastime, especially on weekends. Many experienced climbers come for an outdoor workout while others are still "learning the ropes." There are often families clmbing side by side with hard-core Yosemite veterans.

CLIMBING A-B-Cs

North Berkeley's rocks are collectively a prime location to practice various styles of rock climbing—such as bouldering, top-roping, rappelling, and (occasionally) lead climbing—all within a two-mile radius.

Bouldering involves doing very athletic climbing moves without using ropes or harnesses. The only pieces of equipment required are special climbing shoes with sticky rubber soles and a small waist pouch of white gymnast's chalk, which is used to keep one's hands dry. Typically, boulderers place a thick foam pad called a crash pad under the climb, or "problem," to cushion their fall. This minimalist approach to protection is usually sufficient, as most bouldering problems do not extend very high off of the ground. In the case of more difficult or convoluted problems, another person may "spot"—standing under the problem to catch the falling climber or otherwise help her avoid awkward or dangerous landings. Bouldering problems usually involve very small holds on steep or overhanging sections of rock and focus more on challenging, high-energy individual moves, as opposed to the endurance needed for rope climbing on longer routes.

To some, bouldering is a way of getting fit and keeping fit, improving arm and finger strength, and acquiring technical skill to apply in roped climbing on bigger cliffs like those found in Yosemite. Many rock climbing pioneers and enthusiasts, including David Brower, Galen Rowell, and Arlene Blum, trained for their epic climbs on rocks

in Berkeley. Others consider bouldering the purest form of climbing and have no desire to move on to greater heights. Indian Rock is a perennial favorite among boulderers, perhaps because of the view from the top, but Nat's Traverse, one of the most famous and difficult problems in Berkeley, is on neighboring Mortar Rock.

Top-roping involves climbing with the protection of a rope. This technique is advisable when one is learning to climb or wanting to avoid a ground fall, or if the route is high enough that falling off could be dangerous. To top-rope, a climber rigs a rope at the top of a climb (often by taking an easier route to the top) so that the rope hangs down the face. The climber "ties in" to one end of the rope and his partner, known as the belayer, controls the rope's movement using a small device that arrests the rope in case the climber falls. Because the rope is attached to the rock above the climber, a fall on a top rope is very safe and the climber hardly loses any height. Top-roping is popular on Pinnacle Rock at Remillard Park and at Cragmont Rock Park, two of the highest rock faces in the Berkeley Hills.

Lead climbing involves the security of a rope, but is more precarious than top-roping. As she ascends, the lead climber fastens the rope to pieces of protective gear along the route, or clips in with a carabiner to permanent bolts that are already on the rock at intervals. In the absence of permanent bolts, the second climber removes the protective gear, leaving no trace on the rock. If a climber falls while leading, she falls twice the distance between herself and the last piece of protection she placed, plus any slack in the rope. Usually gear is placed just a few feet apart, minimizing the climber's fall. However, if gear is spaced out too far or if a piece of protection pops out of the rock, the fall can be very long and result in serious injury.

While rappelling (abseiling) is not necessary to descend any of the Berkeley Rocks, since there are easy ways to walk down, many beginning climbers and those who just want the thrill of descending a rock face via sliding down a rope can be seen rappelling at Indian Rock, Cragmont Rock, and Pinnacle Rock.

Climbs are graded, or rated, based on their difficulty, the specific moves involved, and the amount of endurance they require. The Yosemite Decimal System, the grading rubric most common in the U.S., is based on how difficult a climb would be for a lead climber placing protection as he ascends. This system's ratings begin with a five and a decimal point (fifth class indicates use of ropes for protection), followed by a number ranging from one to fifteen, and occasionally a letter between *a* and *d* to further distinguish the difficulty. For example, the hardest route in Berkeley is rated 5.11c according to the guidebook; however, a climber on a top-rope would likely find the climb somewhat easier. Bouldering has its own unique grading method, the John Sherman V-grade system in the U.S., which ranges from V0 to V16. Guidebooks also use stars to indicate the climb's overall quality on a 1 to 5 scale.

FINDING THE ROCKS

NORTH OF BERKELEY

In El Cerrito, **Huber Park** (at the corner of Terrace and Sea View Drives) has immense rock walls dating to the 1930s, and **Canyon Trail Park** (on Conlon Avenue) has natural outcroppings. **Murieta Rock** (at Cutting Boulevard and Arlington) is invisible as you drive by. Turn east on Cutting, however, and you'll find it. Climbing can be dangerous here. Watch out for broken glass. A section of the **Hillside Nature Area** along Moeser Lane across from Sea View Drive has large rock outcrops.

Camp Herms (on Thors Bay Road, above Arlington), a Boy Scout camp, preserves remains of an old rock quarry, as does the **El Cerrito Recycling Center** (at the end of Schmidt Lane past Navellier Street).

The natural rock outcroppings and superb Depression-era stonework at the **Alvarado Staging Area of Wildcat Canyon Regional Park** are worth visiting (parking just past McBryde Avenue at Arlington).

In Kensington, an immense chunk of glaucophane schist can be found in the garden downhill from the Blake mansion at **Blake Garden** (70 Rincon Road).

John Hinkel Park's rustic redwood clubhouse is a fine example of architecture designed to blend in with the natural setting.

BERKELEY

The best map for the Berkeley portion of the East Bay hills is *Berkeley Pathways*, published by the Berkeley Path Wanderers Association and available at most bookstores.

The best way to enjoy the Berkeley Rocks is on foot. Pathways lead from park to park and provide generous glimpses of rock along the way. Wherever you go, notice the stone pillars put in place by developers to advertise their wares.

From the top of Solano Avenue, where it hits The Alameda, **Indian Rock Path** will take you steeply to **Indian Rock Park**, for climbing or views (Indian Rock Avenue at Shattuck Avenue). Around the bend is **Mortar Rock Park**, for climbing and to see mortar holes (Indian Rock Avenue past Oxford Street). Proceed uphill on Indian Rock Avenue, then turn left at Santa Barbara Road to visit **Grotto Rock Park** for views. Nearby **John Hinkel Park** (parking on Somerset Place) is worth visiting to see its stone fireplace. On your way back to Solano, detour onto Contra Costa Avenue to visit **Contra Costa Rock Park** (Contra Costa Avenue north of Solano) for views. Carved stairways provide a route up many of these rocks, but careful stepping is required!

The small **Great Stoneface Park** (Thousand Oaks Boulevard at San Fernando Avenue), a popular spot for picnickers and dog walkers, is best seen while touring Thousand Oaks. Start at the bus stop at Colusa Avenue and Thousand Oaks Boulevard, noticing its rocks, then ramble uphill.

Vincente Avenue is particularly rich with rocks, which can be

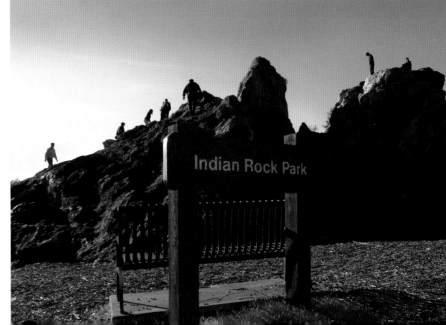

seen beneath, behind, or in front of many homes. The **Visalia Steps** from Vincente Avenue to Menlo Place provide rocky views and lead to **Picnic Rock**, a privately owned city landmark (at Santa Rosa Avenue near Menlo Place). The Alameda has its share of marvelous rocks.

Other streets and pathways worth exploring for rocks are the **Yosemite Steps** between The Alameda and Arlington Avenue, **Thousand Oaks Boulevard** between Colusa and Arlington, and **El Paseo Path** between Vincente and The Alameda. **Indian Trail** is particularly rustic and retains immense concrete urns that were put in place as the neighborhood was just being developed.

Shattuck Avenue and **Oxford Street** on both sides of Marin Avenue have wonderful rocks adorning many homes. Be careful crossing Marin!

Further up the hill, **Easter Way** and **Pinnacle Path** are convenient routes to **Cragmont Rock Park** (Regal Road at Easter Way), with its wonderful picnic grounds, immense rock, and trails, and **Remillard Park** (Keeler Avenue at Poppy Lane), with the imposing **Pinnacle Rock**.

Glendale–La Loma Park (on La Loma Avenue) preserves traces of the quarry it once was.

Founders' Rock is at the southwest corner of Gayley Road and Hearst Avenue, on the University of California campus. South of campus, stone walls can be admired on **Hillside Avenue** and **Hillside Court** near Dwight Way.

Rocks are hard to spot in the Claremont neighborhood due to development. But if you walk—don't try this while driving!—along Tunnel Road, you'll find an immense rock at the corner of **Vicente Road**. The **stone entry gates and bus stop** on Claremont Avenue at the Uplands were designed by John Galen Howard for Duncan McDuffie's Claremont subdivision.

OAKLAND

Robert Sibley Volcanic Regional Preserve provides tours of an extinct volcanic center (Skyline Boulevard just east of Grizzly Peak Boulevard).

Want more rocks? The more you walk, the more you'll find.

RESOURCES

About Stone

http://aboutstone.org

This international, noncommercial information and contact resource for people who work with natural stone hosts the Stone Sculpture Virtual Library and Stone Conversations email discussion group.

Stone Foundation

116 Lovato Lane
Santa Fe, NM 87505
(505) 989-4644
http://stonefoundation.org/membersusa.html

The Stone Foundation's mission is to celebrate stone and stone skills; to preserve and perpetuate the time-honored art and craft of stonework, particularly structural stonework, and encourage and inform the resurgence of interest in it through publications, workshops, seminars, symposia, etc; and to research and communicate the history, traditions, and culture of stonework.

Zach Pine

http://homepage.mac.com/zpine/index.html

A local artist who creates impermanent sculptures using natural materials in outdoor settings.

ORGANIZATIONS

Bay Area Rock Art Conservation and Education Fund

c/o Marin Community Foundation
5 Hamilton Landing, Suite 200
Novato, CA 94949
http://bancroft.berkeley.edu/collections/rockart/barara.html

The BARACEF is a nonprofit charitable trust administered through the Marin Community Foundation. The fund seeks donations from the public in support of projects that further the preservation of Bay Area and Northern California rock art sites.

Berkeley Architectural Heritage Association

2318 Durant Avenue
Berkeley, CA 94704
(510) 841-2242
http://www.berkeleyheritage.com

The Berkeley Architectural Heritage Association promotes, through education, an understanding and appreciation for Berkeley's history, and encourages the preservation of its historic buildings.

Berkeley Historical Society

1931 Center Street
Berkeley, CA 94701
(510) 848-0181
http://www.ci.berkeley.ca.us/histsoc/#HOME

A nonprofit all-volunteer group serving as a primary resource for the collection and preservation of local history and celebrating the diversity of Berkeley's people by keeping the city's history a vital part of residents' lives.

Berkeley Ironworks

800 Potter Street
Berkeley, CA 94710
(510) 981-9900
http://www.touchstoneclimbing.com/bi.html

Among the largest rock climbing gyms in the country, with climbing terrain on hundreds of routes and boulder problems, as well as dozens of group classes for climbers at all skill levels.

Berkeley Path Wanderers Association

1442A Walnut Street, Box 269
Berkeley, CA 94709
http://www.berkeleypaths.org

Dedicated to the creation, preservation, and restoration of public paths, steps, and walkways in Berkeley for the use and enjoyment of all.

Cragmont Climbing Club

http://www.geocities.com/danielzimmerlin

Originally founded in 1932 by rock climbers who were the first to scale Yosemite's cliffs, this organization was officially part of the Sierra Club's Rock Climbing Section for many years. Current club members continue the tradition of climbing, teaching, and conservation through social meetings, a newsletter, and periodic outings to major climbing destinations.

Friends of Five Creeks

1236 Oxford Street
Berkeley, CA 94709
http://www.fivecreeks.org

A group of volunteers who seek to protect and restore the watersheds and aquatic and riparian habitat of the creeks of north Berkeley, Albany, Kensington, southern El Cerrito, and Richmond.

Friends of the Fountain and Walk

P.O. Box 8192
Berkeley, CA 94707

Community-based organization formed in 1996 to rebuild the fountain at the Marin Circle, which was demolished in 1958. Members continue to play a pivotal role in the fountain's maintenance.

Hillside Club

2286 Cedar Street
Berkeley, CA 94709
(510) 848-3227
http://www.hillsideclub.org

Founded in the late nineteenth century to promote good design practices in the Berkeley Hills, the Hillside Club today is a community-based membership organization.

BOOKS / MAPS

41 Walking Tours of Berkeley. Berkeley Architectural Heritage Association, 1986.

A Map of Berkeley Pathways. Berkeley Path Wanderers Association. http://www.berkeleypaths.org.

Black, Tresa. *Rock Climbing the San Francisco Bay Area*. Falcon Guide, Globe Pequot Press, 2002.

Cerny, Susan Dinkelspiel. *Berkeley Landmarks: An Illustrated Guide to Berkeley, California's Architectural Heritage*. Berkeley Architectural Heritage Association, 2001.

Guide to San Francisco Bay Area Creeks: Creeks of the East Bay. http://www.museumca.org/creeks/eastbay.html.

House tour guidebooks. Berkeley Architectural Heritage Association. http://www.berkeleyheritage.com.

Keeler, Charles. *The Simple Home*. San Francisco: Paul Elder, 1904.

Maybeck, Bernard. *Hillside Building*. Illustrated booklet for the Berkeley Hillside Club, 1906.

Thornburg, Jim. *Bay Area Rock: A Climber's Guide*. Potlicker Press, 2001.

Willes, Burl, ed. *Picturing Berkeley: A Postcard History*. Gibbs Smith, 2005.

Wollenburg, Charles. *Berkeley, A City in History*. Lecture series, 2002. http://berkeleypubliclibrary.org/system/historytext.html.

Woodbridge, Sally B. *John Galen Howard and the University of California: The Design of a Great Public University Campus*. University of California Press, 2002.

ROCK PARKS OF BERKELEY

For a map of the rock parks, visit http://www.ci.berkeley.ca.us/parks/parkmap.html.

Contra Costa Rock Park
869-A Contra Costa Avenue
Berkeley, CA 94707

Cragmont Rock Park
960 Regal Road
Berkeley, CA 94708

Glendale–La Loma Park
1339 La Loma Avenue
Berkeley, CA 94708

Great Stoneface Park
1930 Thousand Oaks Boulevard
Berkeley, CA 94707

Grotto Rock Park
879 Santa Barbara Road
Berkeley CA 94707

Indian Rock Park
950 Indian Rock Avenue
Berkeley CA 94707

Mortar Rock Park
901 Indian Rock Avenue
Berkeley, CA 94707

Remillard Park
80 Poppy Lane
Berkeley, CA 94708

EAST BAY REGIONAL PARKS

Alvarado Park in Wildcat Canyon Regional Park
Entrance to Alvarado Area is on Park Avenue, just off of McBryde Avenue in Richmond.
http://www.ebparks.org/parks/wildcat.htm

Robert Sibley Volcanic Regional Preserve
6800 Skyline Boulevard
Oakland, CA 94611
http://www.ebparks.org/parks/sibley.htm

AUTHOR'S NOTE

Berkeley Rocks would not have been possible without the unstinting support and wise guidance of my wife, Kirsty Melville. When she and I first arrived in California in 1994, we stayed for a while in Phil Wood's new house on Norwood Avenue in leafy Kensington, a town tucked into the hills just north of Berkeley. Phil was very proud of this house's stunning setting, especially the giant rocks in the bottom of his garden.

As a rock climber, I have always been captivated with large boulders, forever scanning their faces looking for possible routes of ascent. The photographer in me was equally fascinated by the thought of trying to portray this geological marvel in a creative way. So I took some images of Phil's mighty boulders and gave them to him as a present. He was so taken with the prints he quickly came back to me and said, "What about a book on the rocks of the Berkeley Hills?" Nearly twelve years later his idea has finally come to fruition.

My greatest thanks therefore go to Phil Wood, owner and publisher of Ten Speed Press, for his vision and perseverance with this project. His wife, Winifred, who shares in Phil's passion for all things Berkeley, was also always supportive.

In 1994, I was already very familiar with Berkeley's massive climbing boulders, like Indian Rock and Cragmont Rock, from my days as a dedicated rock climber more than a decade earlier. Not long after we moved to Berkeley, however, we went on a spring tour of the Northbrae houses conducted by the Berkeley Architectural Heritage Association (BAHA). The tour helped me begin to appreciate the rich and unique architectural heritage of the Berkeley Hills, and to see that the story of Berkeley's rocks is intertwined with the story of Berkeley's development, houses, and gardens. I soon realized that to tell this the story properly I would need to enlist other experts.

Dave Weinstein's great knowledge of Bay Area architecture and his writing and research skills have added depth and dimension to this exploration of the Berkeley Rocks. He brought many new rocks to light and teased out rich veins of story from people associated with the rocks.

Dave and I were assisted in the research and writing of the book by many individuals and organizations including: from the Berkeley Architectural Historical Society (BAHA), Susan Cerny, Lesley Emmington Jones, Trish Hawthorne, and Sara Wikander; from the Berkeley Historical Society, John Aronivici and Ken Livingston; from the Berkeley Path Wanderers, Prescott Cole, Jacque Ensign, Paul Grunland, Marty Mertens, Emma Morris, Marilyn Siegel, Susan Schwartz, and Pat De Vito. Other individuals whom we consulted were: Ellen Byrne of the Sierra Club, Ron Crane, Neil Collier, Mel Erskine, Sandi Grant, Barbara Kaplan, David Liu, Malcolm Margolin, Dennis Makishima, Erika Mailman, Barbara and Kim Marienthal, Lin Murphy, Leigh Marymor, John Norcross, Richard Phillips, Zach Pine, Lauri Puchall, Julie Rogers, Paul Rogers, Richard Schwartz, Doris Sloan, Allen Steck, John Stockwell, Jim Thornburg, Herman Trutner, Sally Woodbridge, and Dan Zimmerlin.

We were also assisted by many homeowners, including: George Akerlof and Janet Yellen, Ed and Sallie Arens, Alex Adelman, George Break, Robert Doty, Stephen and Doris Chun, Michael Cohn and Molly Stone, Lee and Lone Coleman, Grace Busche Dafoe, Harry Delmer, Betsy and Steve Dixon, Mimi Frueham, Deborah Friedman, Jerry and Helen Finkelstein, John Fornoff, Mary Ford and Rob Lewis, David Hammond, Red Gillen, Jeff Goldberg and Kirsten Bennet, Mariam Grodzins, L. John Harris, Tyler and Kathy Hoare, I. K. and Fatima Hussain, Christopher Kraebel, Kevin Lee, Joye and Dan Leventhal, Eugene W. Lukes, Robin Miller and Dan Rossi, Alan Sparer and Charlotte Fishmann, Parviz and

C. Ruth Shokat, Tom Singman and Kar Kaufman, Alison Taggart, Walter and Robin Tickner, Don Tieck, David Teece, Robert and Anne Luse, Gordon Rausser, Albin Renauer and Mary Randolph, Bill and Erica Roberts, Dan and Kent Smith, Lois and Conrad Stevenson, Craig and Anne Van Dyke, Eric and Katie Wilson, Lyle York and Matt Wilson, and Henriette Zabin.

Very early in the evolution of the book I became a convert to shooting digitally, so almost all the contemporary images have been acquired in this manner. This has given me the freedom to experiment and push the limits of my digital skills, but at the same time it has been a challenge to stay abreast of the masses of files I generated. I was assisted in this task by Sarah Sewell. I was greatly assisted in the archival photo research by the Berkeley Architectural Heritage Association (BAHA), particularly executive director Anthony Bruce; Jack von Euw and Erica Nordmeier at the Bancroft Library; the Berkeley Historical Society; Donald Baston of the Richmond Museum; Trish Hawthorne; John Stockwell; Steve Lavoie of the Oakland History Room; and John Knox of the Earth Island Institute.

The editing and design team at Ten Speed Press have also done an outstanding job in wrestling this mass of complex information and images into it a well-organized and handsome book. First to my editors, Annie Nelson and more recently in the final crucial stages, Clancy Drake, thank you for the tremendous job you did in dealing with my many piecemeal contributions. Creative director Nancy Austin has brought her great eye and design talent to bear on this project, which was very much appreciated. I would also like to thank Kathy Hashimoto, editor Melissa Moore, copy editor Jasmine Star, Photoshop guru Mona Meisami, proofreader Mike Ashby, and cartographer Bart Wright. Others at Ten Speed who added their creative energies to the book were designer Colleen Cain, production manager Hal Hershey, and publicist Zak Nelson. All this endeavor was ably overseen by editorial director Aaron Wehner and publisher Lorena Jones.

Lastly it's impossible to thank enough all my friends and colleagues who have lived through the process of making this book with me, but I am very grateful for all your hints, suggestions, information, and anecdotes about the rocks. There are, no doubt, many other boulders and stories out there that we missed, and part of me would have happily continued on this quest to unearth and shoot more gems.

www.BerkeleyRocks.com

ADDITIONAL PICTURE AND TEXT CREDITS

Pages 5, 46, and 59 courtesy of the Berkeley Historical Society

Pages 8, 43, 46, 47, 48, and 106 courtesy of Berkeley Architectural Heritage Association

Page 24 courtesy of John Stockwell

Pages 36 and 37 courtesy of The Bancroft Library, University of California, Berkeley

Page 44 courtesy of Anthony Bruce

Page 58 courtesy of the Earth Sciences and Map Library, University of California, Berkeley

Page 114 courtesy of Zach Pine

Page 129 courtesy of the Oakland History Room, Oakland Public Library

Page 139 courtesy of the Richmond Museum of History Collection

Page 144 courtesy of the Brower Family Collection, Earth Island Institute

Page 149: Pinnacle Rock climbing route descriptions were used by permission of FalconGuides, http://falcon.trails.com

The photo on page 160 is an image of Indian Rock.